CITRUS
COOKBOOK

CITRUS COOKBOOK

Tantalizing
Food & Beverage Recipes
from Around the World

FRANK THOMAS
&
MARLENE LEOPOLD

CLEAR LIGHT PUBLISHERS
SANTA FE, NEW MEXICO

ACKNOWLEDGMENTS

First and foremost, we would like to dedicate this book to the memory of Thomas A. Thomas—father, uncle, partner, teacher, and mentor. It was only through his encouragement and inspiration that this book was made possible.

As authors we receive credit for this book, but an undertaking of this magnitude cannot be accomplished in a vacuum. We would therefore like to acknowledge and thank the following named individuals and entities for their part in the completion of this book: Margaret Thomas for her help, ideas, and recipes; Valerie Losio and Anthony Roberti for dedicating (and subjecting) their kitchens to the testing and developing of many of the recipes; and family members, present and past, who taught us respect for food and the love of cooking.

Recipes identified by an * in the title are the property of The Florida Department of Citrus. We wish to express our gratitude to that department for their cooperation and generosity in allowing us to use them.

Clear Light Publishers, 823 Don Diego, Santa Fe, NM 87501
WEB: www.clearlightbooks.com

First Edition
10 9 8 7 6 5 4 3 2 1

Library of Congress Cataloging-in-Publication Data

Thomas, Frank, 1948-
    Citrus cookbook: the art of l'orange cuisine: food & beverage
recipes from around the world / Frank Thomas and Marlene A. Leopold.
        p. cm.
    ISBN 1-57416-056-7
    1. Cookery (Citrus fruits) 2. Cookery, International I. Leopold,
Marlene, 1933- . II. Title.
TX813.C5 T49   2000
641.6'4304—dc21   00-047545
                                                                  CIP

Cover photograph © Marcia Keegan
Cover design by Marcia Keegan & Carol O'Shea
Interior typography and design by Mary Rose
Printed in Canada

TABLE OF CONTENTS

Chapter III   SOUPS

Chapter IV   VEGETABLES & SALADS

Chapter V   MEATS & SEAFOOD

INTRODUCTION

Citrus has been a key ingredient in food preparation for centuries and is utilized in virtually every country in the world. Its substantial health benefits, touted irrefutably by authoritative sources like the American Heart Association, the National Institute of Health, and the American Cancer Society, include reducing the risk of stroke, aiding in the prevention of cancer, maintaining cellular integrity by preserving collagen, and perhaps preventing or lessening the symptoms of the common cold. As research continues, the list of health benefits will undoubtedly grow, but it is what citrus does to taste that has maintained its popularity. Citrus not only imparts a wonderful fresh flavor to foods, but also acts as a natural tenderizer to meat, poultry and fish. It is a combination of these qualities that gives citrus limitless versatility, making it perfect for the preparation of virtually every type of food from appetizers and aperitifs to entrées and desserts.

As we enter a new millennium, citrus too begins a re-birth in worldwide popularity. N.A.F.T.A. and other recent international treaties have substantially increased citrus world trade, insuring that seasonal citrus fruits remain available throughout the year and throughout the world. Government programs like AgLink are assisting citrus producers in developing trade ties with Poland, Latvia, Lithuania and Estonia, while improved international relations with the former Soviet Union and China encourage friendly exchange of cooking concepts and ideas and open a brand new world of opportunities in cooking. Agricultural experiments and discoveries have resulted in new varieties of citrus like the W. Murcott and Fina Sodea Clementine oranges that beckon inventive ideas and invite creative recipes. The age of unified international citrus cooking has just begun, making new and refreshing meal ideas like Middle Eastern Roasted Chicken, Indonesian Lamb Kebabs, and Greek Bacon-Wrapped Shrimp not only simple, but welcome changes from a world seemingly headed for standardization.

So start cooking with an international flavor—treat your family and guests to Ukrainian Homemade Mayonnaise instead of ordinary bottled mayonnaise, or, if you prefer, fresh homemade American style Orange, Berry, or Lime Mayonnaise. They're not only delicious and simple to make, but contain no artificial preservatives, chemicals, or colorings. Real dressings, sauces and salsa like authentic Caesar Dressing, French Hollandaise Sauce, and Mexican Black Bean with Mango Salsa are naturals when you use citrus. Greek Avgolemono, Spanish Gazpacho, and other fantastic soups add to any meal, and sensational salads like Arabian Orange, Onion & Black Olive Salad or Surf & Citrus Salad are as impressive to the eye as they are to the palate. Even outstanding beverages like Strawberry Rhubarb Lemonade or a tropical Tortola Fruit Salad Blend are created with fresh wholesome citrus juice. So join the journey of exploration, make the switch from chemicals to flavor and start cooking with international a-peel.

I

Condiments, Sauces & Dressings

LEMON SPREAD

At our house, the following spread is a lovely companion for tea breads.

¼ cup lemon juice, with pulp
3 large eggs, lightly beaten
2 tablespoons butter, whipped
½ cup sugar
1½ tablespoons lemon rind, finely grated
small sprigs lemon or spearmint mint

Set the butter and mint sprigs aside. Combine all remaining ingredients in top of a double boiler over warm water. Cook, stirring constantly, until thickened. Remove from the heat and blend in the butter. Heap mixture onto small fruit dish or use a small baller to segment, garnish with mint sprigs and chill. Store in refrigerator.

LEMON SOUR CREAM

A dollop of herb-flavored sour cream adds color and flavor to a baked potato or bowl of soup. For variation, substitute your herb of choice for lemon in the following.

½ cup sour cream
¼ teaspoon lemon juice
1 tablespoon chopped lemon grass or mint

Gently fold all ingredients together.
Yield: ½ cup.

LEMON BUTTER
Variation #1

Flavored spreads are increasing in popularity because of the diversity they present. Softened butter/margarine may also be blended with your cheese of choice for additional options.

½ cup butter or margarine, softened
½ cup chopped fresh chives
¼ cup minced fresh parsley
1 tablespoon lemon juice
dash pepper

Stir all the ingredients together well and chill. Serve with warm bread of your choice, cornbread or hot biscuits.
Yield: ½ cup.

LEMON BUTTER
Variation #2

A stump-your-guests treat, drop a pat on pork chops as they come off the grill or serve over baked potatoes. We double the following:

2 tablespoons fresh thyme leaves
1 cup butter, softened
1 teaspoon finely grated lemon rind
1 tablespoon fresh lemon juice

Pulse the butter and thyme several times in a food processor or blender. Add the remaining ingredients and process until the mixture is smooth. Scrape the sides of container as needed. Spoon the butter mixture onto plastic wrap, fold over and roll into log shape, working quickly so the butter does not melt from the heat of your hand. Seal in wrap and refrigerate 4 hours or up to 5 days. Slice to serve. For more casual parties, use melon baller or hand roll to form small orbs and serve in glass bowl with a few thyme leaves around for accent.
*Variations can be made with lemon mint or lemon grass. We omit rind in these variations.
Yield: 1 cup.

LEMON GARLIC MARINADE

Excellent for basting chicken, pork or lamb on the grill (we favor rotisserie but have done all) or as a sauce for baking.

½ cup olive oil
1 cup lemon juice
2 cloves crushed garlic
1 tablespoon crushed oregano leaves
1 teaspoon each salt and pepper

Mix together all of the ingredients. Marinate meat choice for one hour. If baking, sprinkle meat with paprika and bake uncovered at 350° until done (approximately 40 minutes).
Yield: 1½ cups.

LEMON SAUCE WITH HERBS

A must-try for couples in the kitchen, we use this delicate yet rich sauce for grilled veal, lamb or shrimp.

Hint: Do not melt butter before adding to sauce. Do not reheat sauce or it will separate.

½ cup lemon juice
¼ cup fresh thyme, snipped
2 green onions, finely chopped
1 clove garlic, minced
1 cup dry white wine
½ cup whipping cream
1 cup cold butter, cut into 8 pieces
pinch each salt and ground, black pepper

In medium skillet, combine thyme, green onions, garlic and wine; simmer over medium heat 15 minutes or until liquid is reduced. Stir in whipping cream and continue simmering until mixture is again reduced. Remove from heat; add butter, a few pieces at a time, stirring constantly with wire whisk until smooth. It may be necessary to return to heat to melt butter. Pour sauce through a wire strainer into a bowl. Discard solids. Stir in salt, pepper and lemon juice. Serve immediately.
Yield: 1½ cups.

BASIC HOMEMADE MAYONNAISE
(and Flavor Variations)
1 large egg yolk (room temperature)
1 teaspoon lemon juice
½ teaspoon salt
½ cup olive oil
½ cup vegetable oil
½ teaspoon white wine vinegar
¼ teaspoon freshly ground white pepper

In a large bowl, whisk together egg yolk, lemon juice and salt. Slowly add combined oils, whisk in vinegar and pepper. Cover and chill.
Yield: about 1 cup.

Variations on the above are limited only by imagination and personal preferences. Simply modify the Basic Mayonnaise. Here are some delicious examples:

Orange: A favorite for us, this is fabulous when presented in a round, hollowed-out loaf of French or Italian bread, used as a salad bowl. Fill hollow with 1 cup of fruit salad of your choice. Fold the following into the Basic Mayonnaise:
½ cup sour cream
1 teaspoon sugar
2 tablespoons orange juice
salt and freshly ground pepper to taste

Berry: This is magnificent over a fruit salad presented in a melon half. Mix together 1 cup puréed raspberries or blackberries and 1 teaspoon fresh lemon juice. Fold into the mayonnaise.

Lemon or Lime: A marvelous dressing, this adds a superb touch over fish, before baking or grilling. Substitute lemon or lime juice for vinegar in basic recipe and add 2 teaspoons finely grated lemon or lime peel.

UKRAINIAN HOMEMADE MAYONNAISE

Ukrainian homemakers are often independent spirits with self-suffi-
cient tendencies. The following simple but basic recipe is a staple
indicative of their freedom from supermarkets. They consider variation
challenging and fun.

> 1 egg yolk
> 1 cup chilled salad oil
> juice of ¼ lemon wedge
> pinch of salt

Beat the egg yolk with a whisk. Progressively add the oil while
continuously beating until the mixture begins to thicken. Add the
lemon juice and the remainder of the oil pouring in a little at a time.
Add the salt according to taste.
Yield: 1 cup.

LEMON VINAIGRETTE DRESSING

As with mayonnaise options, vinaigrettes can be as diverse as the imag-
ination allows. The ingredients may be combined, covered tightly, shak-
en vigorously and chilled. Never was the adage "Variety is the spice of
life" more fitting. Following are a few of our choices.

> ¼ teaspoon salt
> ½ teaspoon black pepper
> 1 teaspoon Dijon-style mustard
> 1 teaspoon orange blossom honey
> ⅔ cup olive oil
> 2 tablespoons lemon juice
> 1 tablespoon grated lemon peel
> 2 tablespoons white wine vinegar
> 1 tablespoon chopped fresh lemon verbena, if available

In a small bowl, blend together the salt, pepper, mustard, honey and
olive oil. Whisk in the lemon juice, grated peel, chopped lemon
verbena and wine vinegar. As the mixture is whisked it will lightly
thicken and become cloudy. Once blended, cover and refrigerate
until needed.
Yield: Approximately ⅔ cup.

LEMON HONEY

½ cup fresh lemon balm or lemon verbena
1 cup orange blossom honey

Coarsely chop the lemon herbs and place them in a saucepan with honey. Cook the mixture over low heat for 15 minutes. Pour through wire-mesh strainer; discard the solids. Store on shelf in sealed jar.
Yield: 1½ cups.

LEMON-HONEY VINAIGRETTE

1 cup white wine vinegar
¾ cup vegetable oil
¼ cup honey of choice
1 tablespoon grated lemon rind
3 tablespoons fresh lemon juice
1 teaspoon salt
2 cloves garlic, minced

Mix all ingredients together until thoroughly blended.
Yield: 2 cups.

ORANGE & SESAME SEED DRESSING

1 teaspoon tarragon and thyme mustard
¼ teaspoon salt
½ teaspoon freshly ground black pepper
1 teaspoon finely grated orange peel
½ cup sesame oil
2 tablespoons fresh orange juice
1 tablespoon sesame seeds
1 tablespoon chopped fresh tarragon
2 teaspoons chopped fresh thyme

Blend together mustard, salt, pepper, orange peel and sesame oil. Whisk in the orange juice and sesame seeds. As the mixture is whisked it will thicken and become cloudy. When blended well cover and refrigerate until needed. Stir in the chopped herbs before serving.
Yield: ⅔ cup.

GRAPEFRUIT VINAIGRETTE DRESSING

½ cup grapefruit juice
⅓ cup white wine vinegar
⅓ cup vegetable oil
1 clove garlic, minced
2 tablespoons bottled capers, drained
1 tablespoon Dijon-style mustard
1¼ teaspoons dried leaf tarragon, crumbled
½ teaspoon salt
¼ teaspoon pepper

Mix all ingredients well in a medium mixing bowl. Cover tightly and refrigerate until needed.
Yield: Approximately 1¼ cups.

LEMON COCKTAIL SAUCE

Incredibly refreshing over most seafood cocktails. We favor crab and shrimp but any will work.

⅔ cup homemade mayonnaise
2 teaspoons horseradish
2 teaspoons snipped lemon grass
1 teaspoon yellow mustard
3 tablespoons lemon juice

Mix together and chill before serving. Garnish with lemon slices.
Yield: ⅔ cup.

PARSLEY SAUCE

Superb over seafood or boiled potatoes. Attractive when garnished with mint sprigs or lemon twists.

¼ cup melted butter
3 tablespoons lemon juice
¼ cup chopped parsley

In a small saucepan, combine all of the ingredients and warm over low heat. Serve still warm.
Yield: ⅔ cup.

TARRAGON CREAMY DRESSING

Try this over your favorite seafood salad. We prefer it drizzled over shrimp and/or crab but it will complement most seafood choices. Serve with a basket of orange muffins and herb butters.

1 tablespoon flour
2 tablespoons granulated sugar
dash each salt and black pepper
½ teaspoon tarragon vinegar
⅓ cup lemon juice
2 tablespoons olive oil
2 eggs, beaten
1½ cups evaporated milk
1 tablespoon chopped lemon balm or parsley

Slowly combine together the flour, sugar, salt and vinegar in a small saucepan. Continue stirring while slowly adding the oil, eggs and lemon juice. Simmer until the mixture thickens. Remove from the heat and add milk, then beat until smooth. Pour into a gravy boat, sprinkle with chopped lemon balm and chill.
Yield: 8 servings.

RAISIN SAUCE FOR COUNTRY HAM

2 cups red raisins
1½ cups water
pinch salt
2 cups sugar
1 tablespoon cornstarch
1 tablespoon grated orange rind
3 tablespoons fresh orange juice
½ cup chopped walnuts or pecans (optional)

In medium saucepan, bring raisins, water and salt to a boil, then reduce the heat and simmer for 30 minutes. Combine the sugar, cornstarch, orange juice and rind, in the mixture, mix well and bring to a boil, stirring constantly. Boil for 1 minute while stirring constantly then remove from heat. Stir in nuts if desired.
Yield: 2 cups.

ORANGE VINAIGRETTE

⅔ cup olive oil
⅓ cup red wine vinegar
½ teaspoon grated orange rind
1½ teaspoons fresh orange juice
½ teaspoon salt
¼ teaspoon poppy seeds
⅛ teaspoon pepper

Mix all ingredients together until thoroughly blended.
Yield: 1 cup.

VIETNAMESE LIME DIPPING SAUCE

Traditional Vietnamese cooking usually contains dipping sauces with fish sauce. This can be confusing to the uninitiated until you understand that fish sauce is the Vietnamese version of salt or soy sauce. The following is an example.

1 clove garlic, crushed
1 fresh red chile, seeded and crushed
¼ cup sugar
¼ cup lime juice, including pulp
3 tablespoons fish sauce
½ cup water

Combine and mix well all of the ingredients in a small bowl with a tight lid. Serve with fish or egg rolls.
Yield: Approximately 1 cup.

DRIED CITRUS PEEL

The virtues of dried citrus peel cannot be over stated. The task is simple enough and well worth the effort.

6 citrus fruits of aromatic varieties (lemon, lime & orange)

Peel the rind in thin layers and oven dry at 200° for 6 hours. (Sun drying for 2 days may be used in arid climates). Store peels in a tight container, preferably on a cool, dry shelf, away from light. Do not refrigerate. Grind just before using.

BONNE AMIE DRESSING

We consider foods that can be prepared ahead to be good friends, as advanced preparation frees us to focus on the last-minute details of the meal. In this "Good Friend" dressing, 24-hour-ahead preparation not only provides additional time but allows delicate flavors to blend and permeate before serving. Use caution, however, as allowing it to sit beyond a 3-day period will invite loss of flavor.

    ¼ cup hot water
    2 tablespoons capers
    ⅓ fresh dill weed, chopped
    1½ cups fresh parsley, chopped
    3 tablespoons fresh lemon juice
    1 teaspoon lemon peel, finely grated
    2 shallots, sliced
    1 garlic cloves, halved
    2 teaspoons mustard, Dijon style
    ¼ teaspoon salt
    ½ teaspoon coarsely ground black pepper
    ⅔ cup olive oil

Setting oil aside, combine all other ingredients in a blender container. Blend until smooth. On high speed, gradually add the oil in a steady stream and process until the mixture begins to thicken. Tightly cover and chill in the refrigerator. Serve over green salad of choice and garnish with finely grated lemon rind.

LEMON SALT

For the health-conscious gourmet, the hazards of commercial spice combinations, especially salt and pepper variations, can be avoided with an investment of time.

Hint: An excellent seasoning for poultry and fish.
    1 tablespoon ground dried lemon peel
    1 tablespoon allspice
    ½ tablespoon sea salt crystals (adjust amount to taste)

Use a pestle and mortar for this mixing task.

ORANGE GLAZE

A refreshing choice for baked ham.

> 3 tablespoons light brown sugar
> 1 teaspoon yellow mustard
> ½ cup fresh orange juice
> ¼ teaspoon cinnamon, finely ground
> 1 teaspoon orange rind, finely grated
> 1 orange, sliced

Set aside the orange slices. In a small saucepan, heat all of the remaining ingredients until the sugar is dissolved and the syrup is slightly thickened. Cool and set aside to apply to scored baked ham. Arrange slices over top of ham and brush on in several applications during the final 20 minutes of baking.

BARBEQUE SAUCE

Something different and a tangy favorite with teenagers, toss in cooked vermicelli for the best of two worlds.

> 1 cup catsup
> ¼ cup apple vinegar
> 1 tablespoon yellow mustard
> 1 tablespoon Worcestershire sauce
> 1 cup brown sugar
> 6 ounces fresh orange or lemon juice, with pulp
> 1 small sweet onion, minced
> 1 tablespoon vegetable oil

In small saucepan, sauté minced onion in oil. Add all of the ingredients and bring to a boil, then simmer for 20 minutes. Cover and chill. Serve as basting sauce for any meat or fish.
Yield: 2 cups.

QUICK & PERFECT HOLLANDAISE SAUCE

Ideal for the gourmet cook with little time and much desire. Try on eggs or vegetables.

> 2 egg yolks
> ¼ teaspoon salt
> ¼ teaspoon hot pepper sauce
> ½ cup warm melted butter
> 3 tablespoons lemon juice

Beat the yolks until thick and lemon colored; add the salt and hot pepper sauce. Add butter in a steady stream while beating constantly. Stir in the lemon juice in a steady stream, beating constantly.
Yield: ½ cup.

A popular variation of Hollandaise Sauce is the California version. Simply add 1½ tablespoons orange juice and 1½ teaspoons grated orange rind to approximately ⅔ cup of the basic Hollandaise Sauce. Especially invigorating over cooked vegetables.

II

APPETIZERS

SAGANAKI
(Flaming Cheese with Lemon)

The Greeks have a dramatic flair for presentation unequaled in the world. Imagine your guests' expressions when you serve them a platter of flaming cheese and extinguish the flame by squeezing a lemon-half over it. Try Saganaki for a preface that's hard to beat.

Hint: Though Romano is sometimes used as a substitute for Kasseri when grated cheese is called for, its use here will lose something. Don't risk it!

> 1 pound Kasseri cheese, sliced into 1" strips
> 2 ounces brandy
> 2 large lemons, halved and seeded
> ½ cup olive oil
> yolk of 2 eggs
> ½ cup flour
> ½ cup bread crumbs

Slice the kasseri into even strips. Use tongs to dip strips in rotating fashion from flour to egg yolk to bread crumbs, coating lightly on all sides. Brown in hot olive oil, turning only once. Use a slotted utensil to lift and arrange on a metal serving platter. Sprinkle cheese with brandy and CAREFULLY ignite. In full view of guests, extinguish the flame with a pass of lemon halves over the platter, squeezing juice onto flame. Supply wooden picks and serve immediately.
Yield: 12 servings.

WATEA EENAB (ARABIC)
(Stuffed Grapevine Leaves)

Stuffed grapevine leaves require an appreciation for the unique. Once acquired, they command loyalty that has no equal. In small portions, it is appropriate as a finger-food appetizer, or in larger portions as the main course. Either way will distinguish you among hosts.

The Greek and Arabic variations are provided below to illustrate the different preparation styles of the cultures; Frank's modern approach using a pressure cooker has also been included.

Hints:
1. In the Arabic version, the secret is in the abundant use of lemon. Don't skimp!
2. If using leaves preserved in brine, omit salt from stuffing. Fresh leaves require salt.
3. Traditionally lamb is used in the stuffing; however, many Arab-Americans prefer beef. Let preference dictate.

>   1 cup white rice, uncooked
>   1 pound diced or ground lamb or beef
>   2 tablespoons melted butter
>   ½ teaspoon ground cinnamon
>   1 tablespoon salt (optional)
>   1 teaspoon ground black pepper
>   ½ cup lemon juice
>   20 grapevine leaves
>   1 large lemon, halved

Hushway (filling): Mix meat of choice, butter, rice and spices together. Set aside.

Rinse grapevine leaves in cold water and set aside on paper towels to drain. Trim stem from each leaf and place on counter, back side up. Set aside large-veined or torn leaves. These will be used to line kettle later. Place a small amount of filling (approximately 1 tablespoon) at large end of leaf and begin rolling away from you, folding both ends in before final roll. Keep the roll neat, remembering that rice will swell as it absorbs liquid during cooking. The finished roll will resemble a cigar. Continue until all of mixture has been rolled. Line kettle with lamb bones and/or leaves and line up rolls, side by side until bottom of kettle is covered. Line up second layer in the opposite direction to permit easy removal after

cooking. Place a heat resistant plate atop to hold the rolls in place and minimize breakage. Add lemon juice and enough water to cover the plate. Simmer, covered, for approximately 45 minutes. Remove from heat and do not lift lid for 10 minutes, permitting rice to steam thoroughly. Remove lid and plate. Carefully, using tongs, transfer grapevine leaves to serving platter and squeeze fresh lemon halves over, just before serving.
Yield: 4 servings.

DOLMATHES (GREEK)
(Stuffed Grapevine Leaves)

    1 pound ground beef
    1 cup white rice, uncooked
    1 medium onion, diced
    1 tablespoon dill weed
    20 grapevine leaves
    2 cups water
    2 tablespoons butter
    lettuce leaves
    salt and pepper to taste

Mix together meat, rice, onion and spices. Trim stem from leaves, if necessary.

    Rinse and separate grapevine leaves in cold water. Line heavy dutch oven or large pot with lettuce leaves. Place a tablespoon (more or less depending on leaf size) of filling in center of leaf, fold in ends and roll from wide end to point. Place in lined pot. When all leaves are rolled, cover with water and distribute butter, cut into chunks, over leaves. Place an oven-proof plate on top to keep the dolmathes in place during cooking. Cover the pot, bring to boil and simmer for 1 hour. Serve with egg/lemon sauce.

Egg/Lemon Sauce:

    4 fresh eggs
    juice from 2 lemons
    hot juice from cooked dolmathes

Beat eggs in a medium-size bowl. While continually beating, slowly add lemon juice and then hot juice from cooked dolmathes. Mix quickly, pour sauce over dolmathes and serve immediately.
Yield: 4 servings.

FRANK'S STUFFED GRAPEVINE LEAVES

Our grandfathers had grape vineyards that they cultured more for the leaves than the grapes. As a child, I remember the leaves being boiled to sterilize them before packing them in brine for preservation. Today they can be bought packed in brine and ready to be stuffed.

   ½ pound ground chuck
   1 cup pearl rice, uncooked
   2 fresh lemons
   ½ teaspoon allspice
   1 jar grapevine leaves
   salt and pepper
   ¼ teaspoon cinnamon

Place the ground beef in a large mixing bowl and add the rice, cinnamon, allspice, salt and pepper, then mix thoroughly until the mixture is well blended. Under cool running water, wash the brine from the grapevine leaves and lay them flat on table, dark side (tops of the leaves) down. Place approximately 1 tablespoon (more or less) of filling onto the base of each leaf and roll into a cigar shape. As they are done place them on the rack in a pressure cooker. When finished add 1 cup of water to the cooker and squeeze the juice from one of the lemons over the grapevine leaves. Place the top on the pressure cooker and cook under pressure for 10 minutes. When the time has expired, cool the cooker instantly by holding it under cold running water, then transfer the grapevine leaves onto a large serving platter. Squeeze lemon juice over the top and garnish with lemon wedges. **Yield: 3 servings.**

IFTOYEER
(Spinach Pies)

Though originating in the Middle East, the spinach pie is a popular choice in western cultures, even finding its way to American lunch boxes and appetizer platters.

   1 pound baby-leaf spinach, chopped
   1 large onion, minced
   ½ cup lemon juice
   2 tablespoons olive oil
   ½ teaspoon each salt and pepper
   dash allspice

½ teaspoon garlic, granulated
½ cup walnuts, chopped, or white raisins (optional)
1 pound white bread dough (available at bakeries or bakery
　　section of food store)

Chop spinach into small pieces. Squeeze spinach to remove all water.
(Aunt Julia stresses the importance of this step especially if frozen
spinach is used.) Mix with onions, spices, oil and lemon juice. Cover
and chill in refrigerator, to wilt and absorb lemon, for 2 hours.
Either walnuts or raisins are added at this time.

　　Roll out bread dough and cut into squares of desired size, then
halved diagonally, to form triangles. Drop 1 tablespoon of mixture
into center of square and fold points to center, closing edges
together. Arrange on a cookie sheet, brush with olive oil and bake at
350º for 15 minutes or until golden.
Yield: 12 pies.

TARATOORA
(Sesame Sauce)

*An integral part of Hummus and Baba Ghannooj, sesame sauce can
also serve as a dipping sauce with baked fish or fried vegetables. Aunt
Betty remembers her parents serving this when they had fish for dinner.*

　　3 cloves garlic, diced
　　½ cup fresh lemon juice
　　½ cup cold water
　　1 cup tahini paste
　　pinch salt

In a large bowl, mash garlic; stir in tahini. Constantly whisking, add
lemon juice and water, a little at a time. Beat until mixture thickens.
Adjust flavor to suit.
Yield: 2 cups.
Variation: A tropical change to the tahini dip is to add peeled and
mashed ripe avocado flesh to the basic sauce.

HUMMUS TAHINI
(Cold Chickpea/Garlic Purée)

A Middle Eastern appetizer that is healthy, delicious and hostess friendly. Make it ahead.

> 1 can chickpeas (garbanzo beans)
> 2 lemons
> 1 cup tahini paste
> 2 garlic cloves, minced
> 2 tablespoons olive oil

Drain the chickpeas and mash them in a mixing bowl. Add the juice from half the lemon, olive oil, tahini paste, and garlic. Mix the ingredients well in a blender or food processor until it forms a thick paste. Add a few drops of water if paste is too thick. Place in a serving bowl and garnish the edges with lemon wedges. Serve with fresh vegetables or fresh pita bread.
Yield: 2 cups.

BABA GHANNOOJ
(Eggplant with Tahini Spread)

There are several ways to cook eggplant. Though the traditional method for baba ghannooj is to broil or cook it over an open fire, we prefer to bake it whole. A popular Middle Eastern appetizer, Baba Ghannooj boasts traditional sesame seed paste (tahini) and lemon juice. Though several variations exist throughout the Arab world, those two constants make it ethnically recognizable.

> 3 small eggplants
> 6 garlic cloves, peeled and finely chopped
> 1 medium onion, quartered
> ½ cup olive oil
> ¼ cup fresh lemon juice
> 2 tablespoons tahini paste
> pinch salt
> 1 tablespoon parsley, finely chopped
> 1 lemon, sliced
> 2 drops hot pepper sauce (optional)
> spearmint or lemon mint sprigs

Preheat oven to 325°. Pierce skin of eggplants in several places to allow steam to escape and bake until cooked through, about 40 minutes. Remove from oven and set aside to cool. Combine all other ingredients in blender and pulse until smooth. Peel and chop cooled eggplants; add to blender mixture; pulse until well mixed. Drizzle with olive oil and chill in deep, glass bowl. Garnish with mint sprigs and lemon slices. Serve with a basket of pita bread.
Yield: 3 Cups.

STUFFED MUSHROOMS

Always the #1 favorite at our holiday buffets, stuffed mushrooms are easily prepared in standard or microwave ovens. The key to the following recipe is to use lemon generously. Garnish with lemon twists and you'll be the envy of the neighborhood.

1½ pounds fresh mushrooms
4 tablespoons butter
2 tablespoons vegetable oil
¾ cup finely diced onions
½ cup lemon juice
1 lemon, quartered
dash each salt and pepper
4 tablespoons chopped parsley
parsley sprigs
½ cup bread crumbs
¼ cup finely grated Romano cheese

Remove stems from mushroom caps. Wash and drain both. Reserve the caps and dice the stems. Into a medium frying pan, add 2 tablespoons butter, ½ tablespoon oil and sauté onions until just golden. Add ¼ cup lemon juice, salt, pepper and stems. Cook slowly until nearly dry, stirring constantly. Remove from heat. Mix in parsley, bread crumbs and cheese. Fill mushroom caps with mixture and arrange in shallow pan coated with nonstick spray. Drizzle remaining butter and lemon juice over tops. Squeeze 2 lemon wedges over caps. Bake 10 minutes at 350°. Garnish serving platter with parsley sprigs and lemon twists. Pass remaining 2 lemon wedges over platter, squeezing juice atop. Serve immediately.
Yield: 6 servings.

LEMON-SALTED PRETZELS

Soft pretzels are a favorite with our card playing friends but good anytime. Try the following for a change.

6 soft pretzels, frozen
2 tablespoons lemon salt (*See* Condiments chapter.)
1 teaspoon lemon juice

Preheat oven to 400°. Arrange frozen soft pretzels on cookie sheet lined with foil. Prepare homemade lemon salt. Remove pretzels from oven and brush with lemon juice. Sprinkle moistened surface with lemon salt. Serve immediately with assortment of mustard varieties. **Yield: 6 servings.**

NORWEGIAN SMOKED SALMON WITH BASIL & KEY LIME

Delicious is only half the praise describing this appetizer. It is an extremely attractive dish with bright brilliant colors that, when arranged on white or monochrome pastel plates, appears more elaborate than it really is. Complimentary colored napkins add to the sensation.

2 raw smoked salmon slices
1 tablespoon fresh basil
2 key limes
8 ounces pitted black olives
4 romaine leaves, well shaped
salt and pepper to taste

Wash the romaine leaves and pat them dry on a paper towel. Drain black olives and set aside. Cover the bottom of an attractive serving platter with romaine leaves and arrange the salmon slices on top of the lettuce. Generously sprinkle chopped basil on each salmon slice and squeeze the juice from one key lime onto the slices. Cut the remaining lime into slivers and distribute on top of the salmon slices. Sprinkle with salt and pepper and serve cold. A random array of pitted black olives around the platter adds color contrast to the presentation.
Yield: 4 servings.

BROILED GRAPEFRUIT

Having had grapefruit only chilled, the first time I was served broiled grapefruit, I was certain the chef had made an error. Instead, the experience revealed to me the astonishing succulence added by the heating of citrus.

 2 large grapefruit, halved with visible seeds removed
 4 tablespoons brown sugar
 1 chicken liver, quartered
 1 tablespoon butter

Cut grapefruit in half. Section with citrus knife, loosening each wedge from its membrane. Remove center. Place halves on broiling pan. Smooth 1 tablespoon of brown sugar over each half. Sauté chicken livers in butter for 2 minutes. Place sautéed chunk of chicken liver in center of each grapefruit half. Slide under broiler until sugar bubbles and fruit/liver begins to blister and brown. Serve directly.
Yield: 4 servings.

CANTALOUPE FRAPPÉ

An icy cold, almost frozen, before-meal treat containing only fresh natural ingredients and no refined sugar. A perfect prelude to lunch or dinner on those hot muggy days of summer.

 1 large ripe cantaloupe
 4 tablespoons honey
 2 tablespoons lemon juice
 fresh mint leaves
 ½ cup dry sherry

Peel the cantaloupe and remove all of the seeds, then slice it into small chunks. Place approximately half the cantaloupe pieces in a food processor or blender and purée them, then pour the pulp into a large mixing bowl. Add the honey, sherry, lemon juice, and the remaining half of the cantaloupe chunks and stir gently but well. Place the mixture into the refrigerator to chill for a minimum of three hours. It is vital to leave the mixture in the refrigerator or freezer until it has chilled through. With this in mind, allow enough time for preparation. Top with mint leaves and serve.
Yield: 4 servings.

SPANISH BAKED OYSTERS WITH PORT WINE CHEESE & PARSLEY

Oysters on your mind? How about oysters baked fresh and hot, and smothered in a blanket of unique port wine cheese, then topped with fresh parsley. Oyster lovers should beware though: This recipe is habit forming!

> 8 ounces shredded port wine cheese
> 1 dozen fresh oysters, shelled
> crisp crackers
> several sprigs fresh parsley
> 1 fresh lemon, cut into wedges

Preheat the oven to 350°. Using an oyster knife, carefully work the blade between the upper and lower shells on the unhinged side of the shell until it penetrates the inside of the oyster. Draw the knife the full length of the oyster side severing all portions that hold the shells together. Remove and discard the top shells leaving the oyster meat resting in the bottom half shell. Place the oysters in a shallow baking dish prepared with nonstick cooking spray, shell side down. Sprinkle bits of cheese and parsley over oysters. When all of the oysters have been coated place them in the preheated oven for 15 minutes or until the edges of the oysters curl and all of the cheese is melted. Remove the oysters from the baking dish and arrange them in a single layer on a serving platter leaving room in the center for a mound of crackers. For an elegant look and to provide a sprinkle of tang for those desiring it, place the lemon wedges around the plate's rim.
Yield: 4 Servings.

SOUTH-OF-THE-BORDER BLACK BEAN WITH MANGO SALSA

Between the strong Hispanic influence in Florida and the thriving citrus industry, citrus and salsa seem an ideal partnership.

> 2 15¾-ounce cans black beans, drained and rinsed
> 2 oranges, peeled, seeded and chopped
> 2 mangos, peeled, pitted and chopped
> ½ sweet red pepper, cored, seeded and chopped
> 3 serrano chiles, or 1 large jalapeño chile, seeded and thinly sliced
> 2 tablespoons fresh lime juice
> 2 tablespoons chopped fresh cilantro
> 1 teaspoon grated fresh ginger

Combine all ingredients in a large mixing bowl and mix well. Tightly cover and place the mixture in the refrigerator for several hours or overnight. Serve with hot tortilla chips or chunks of Cuban or French bread to please the most finicky of appetites.
Yield: 8 cups.

CLAMS CASINO

The sweet smoky taste of bacon and the crunchiness of fresh green peppers form a perfect partnership that undoubtedly accounts for its longevity in popularity. If you're in search of adventure, try using red bell peppers and chopped onion in place of green peppers.

> 1 dozen fresh clams
> ½ cup fresh green pepper, minced
> ½ cup bacon, minced
> 1 tablespoon lemon juice
> fresh ground black pepper

Preheat the oven to 450°. Drain the clams well and remove any shell fragments. Remove the top shell leaving the clam in the lower half shell. Arrange the clams on a cooking platter prepared with nonstick spray, shell side down. Distribute a portion of green pepper, lemon juice, bacon, and fresh pepper, over each clam. When each has been coated, place them into the oven and bake for approximately 10 minutes or until the edges appear crisp. Serve immediately.
Yield: 4 servings.

LIME GUACAMOLE

Avocado and lime fit one another like hand and glove. A popular Mexican dip, guacamole is well suited to Florida since avocados and limes grow here in abundance. Keep in mind that lemon works equally well in the following basic recipe and remains authentic.

Hint: Guacamole is often used as a garnish to other Mexican dishes.

    2 large avocados
    2 cloves garlic, minced
    1 small jalapeño pepper, seeded and minced
    juice of 2 limes, with pulp
    1 vine-ripened tomato, seeded and chopped (optional)
    1 teaspoon salt
    2 twists fresh ground black pepper
    1 lime, sliced

Peel avocado and set seed aside. Mash flesh in large bowl with tight lid.
    Mix together all ingredients and submerge seeds into mixture. (This will help it retain fresh green appearance.) Refrigerate for at least 3 hours. Remove seeds before serving; and stir.
    Garnish with lime slices and serve with basket of tortilla chips or crackers.
Yield: 1 pint.

*FIVE-SPICE APPETIZER MEATBALLS

Turn these miniature meatballs into a main dish by spooning several meatballs and sauce over hot cooked rice or noodles.

    1 slightly beaten egg white
    ¾ cup soft bread crumbs
    ¼ teaspoon five-spice powder
    1 pound lean ground beef
    1½ cups Florida orange juice
    3 tablespoons honey
    4 teaspoons cornstarch
    4 teaspoons soy sauce
    ¼ teaspoon ground ginger
    1 medium red and/or green sweet pepper, cut into 1-inch pieces

In a large bowl combine egg white, bread crumbs, five-spice powder, and ½ teaspoon salt. Add beef; mix well. Shape into 48 1-inch meatballs. Place in a 15- by 10- by 1-inch baking pan. Bake in a 350° oven for 15 to 20 minutes or until no pink remains in center of meatballs. Drain.

Meanwhile, in a large saucepan stir together orange juice, honey, cornstarch, soy sauce, and ginger. Cook and stir until thickened and bubbly. Cook and stir for 2 minutes more. Add sweet pepper and meatballs in saucepan; cook and stir until heated through. Keep warm in a fondue pot or chafing dish. Serve with toothpicks.
Yield: 48 appetizer-size meatballs.

*HOT CRAB DIP

Pita chips are great low-fat dippers for this scrumptious dip. To make the chips, cut 4 pita rounds in half horizontally. Cut each half into 6 wedges. Place in a single layer on an ungreased baking sheet. Bake in a 350° oven 8 to 10 minutes or until crisp.

nonstick spray coating
1 cup chopped fresh mushrooms
¾ cup Florida Orange Juice
1 14-ounce can artichoke hearts, well-drained and chopped
⅔ cup fat-free mayonnaise dressing
⅓ cup sliced green onions
⅓ cup grated Parmesan cheese
¼ cup diced pimiento
1 6-ounce can lump crabmeat, drained, flaked, and cartilage removed

Spray an unheated medium saucepan with nonstick coating. Heat over medium-high heat. Add mushrooms; cook and stir until tender. Remove from heat. Add orange juice, artichokes, mayonnaise dressing, onions, cheese, and pimiento. Gently fold in crabmeat. Transfer to a 1-quart casserole.

Bake, uncovered, in a 400° oven for 20 to 25 minutes or until bubbly. Cool for 5 minutes. Stir before serving. Serve warm with pita chips, vegetable dippers, or assorted crackers. Makes about 3½ cups.
Yield: 12 servings.

*ZESTY MEATBALLS

Cook and serve this appetizer from your crockery cooker.

Hint for shaping meatballs: On a piece of waxed paper, pat the ground meat mixture into a square. Divide meat into the number of meatballs needed by cutting into smaller squares (5 cuts crosswise and 5 lengthwise for 36 meatballs). Roll each square into a ball.

> 1 cup bottled barbecue sauce
> ¾ cup frozen Florida orange juice concentrate,
>   thawed
> 1 beaten egg white
> ¾ cup graham cracker crumbs
> 3 tablespoons milk
> 2 teaspoons prepared mustard
> ¼ teaspoon salt
> 12 ounces lean ground beef
> 12 ounces ground raw turkey or chicken
> nonstick spray coating

In a 3½- or 4-quart crockery cooker stir together barbecue sauce and thawed concentrate; set aside.

For meatballs, in a large mixing bowl combine egg white, cracker crumbs, milk, mustard, salt, and ⅛ teaspoon pepper. Add beef and turkey; mix well. Shape into 36 meatballs (*See* tip, above.).

Spray an unheated 12-inch skillet with nonstick coating. Add meatballs and brown on all sides over medium heat. (Or, place meatballs in a 15- by 10- by 1-inch baking pan. Bake in a 375° oven about 20 minutes or until no pink remains.) Drain meatballs; transfer to crockery cooker. Spoon sauce mixture over meatballs. Cover and cook on low-heat setting for 4 to 5 hours or on high-heat setting for 1½ to 2 hours. Serve with wooden picks.
Yield: 36 meatballs.

Oven Meatballs Variation: Prepare meatballs as above, except add ¼ cup water to the sauce mixture. After browning meatballs, place them in a 2-quart casserole. Pour sauce mixture over meatballs. Cover and bake the meatballs in a 350° oven for 1 hour.

*ORANGE JALAPEÑO CHICKEN PARTY PINWHEELS

    1 package 10-inch flour tortillas (6 tortillas)
    8 ounces cream cheese, softened
    1 tablespoon jalapeño chiles, chopped
    2 tablespoons orange marmalade
    1 tablespoon green onions, chopped
    1 tablespoon fresh parsley, chopped
    4 baked or grilled chicken breasts, cut in thin strips
    2 cups fresh spinach, cut in very thin strips
    1 avocado, sliced
    Grapefruit Salsa (*See* recipe, below.)

Mix softened cream cheese with jalapeño chiles, orange marmalade, green onions and parsley. Spread on middle of flour tortillas, making sure to leave at least a half inch around edge. Top with several thin chicken strips. Top with avocado and shredded spinach. Top with dollop of salsa.

    Roll tortillas and refrigerate until chilled (approximately 4 hours). Cut tortillas into 1 inch slices. Arrange on plate and garnish with Florida citrus fruit.
Yield: Approximately 48 pinwheels.

*GRAPEFRUIT SALSA

    1 cup pink Florida grapefruit, sections
    1 cup white Florida grapefruit, sections
    2 tablespoons green onions, chopped
    2 tablespoons fresh parsley, minced
    2 tablespoons raspberry vinegar
    2 teaspoons brown sugar
    2 tablespoons chile sauce
    2 drops Tabasco sauce
    black pepper, Lawry's seasoning salt, and rum to taste

*SANIBEL SUNSHINE APPETIZER

This is a tasty variation of the traditional shrimp cocktail with a little zip thanks to the avocado, grapefruit and chile sauce.

> 4 fresh Florida grapefruit
> 18 cooked, cleaned shrimp
> 1 medium avocado, peeled and cut in ½-inch cubes
> 1 cup bottled chile sauce
> 1 tablespoon prepared horseradish
> ¼ cup diced red onion
> ¼ cup diced green pepper
> ¼ cup sliced celery
> Lettuce leaves to line grapefruit shells

Cut each grapefruit in half and remove sections, placing them in a large non-metal mixing bowl. Scrape out 6 of the grapefruit halves and set them aside. Cut shrimp in half lengthwise; add to grapefruit in bowl. Add avocado cubes to bowl. In another bowl, combine chile sauce, horseradish, onion, green pepper and celery. Mix well and add to bowl; toss gently. Line the 6 grapefruit shells with lettuce and mound the grapefruit mixture in them.
Yield: 6 servings.

SOUPS

GREEK AVGOLEMONO

This is unquestionably one of our favorites. The tart taste of fresh lemon infuses otherwise ordinary chicken and rice with extraordinary taste. If you enjoy the hint of fresh lemon, you'll love this delicious characteristically Greek soup.

    1 3-pound stewing chicken
    1 cup rice, uncooked
    3 large eggs
    ¼ cup fresh lemon juice
    celery leaves
    2 quarts water
    salt and pepper

Cut the stewing chicken into pieces and place them in a large cooking pot. Add 2 quarts of water to the pot with 1 tablespoon of salt, and the celery leaves. On low heat simmer the chicken for about 2 hours or until it is cooked through and tender, then let the mixture cool. Remove the chicken pieces from the stock, strip off 1½ cups of meat chopping it into small pieces. Bring 6 cups of the chicken stock to a boil in a large pot. Once boiling, add the rice and stir well. Separate the eggs, beating the whites until stiff; the yolks only slightly. Fold the yolks gently into the egg whites along with the lemon juice. When rice is done, add the egg mixture to it slowly while stirring gently. Add the chicken pieces and serve hot with a basket of crusty bread.
Yield: 6 servings.

BASIC CHICKEN & RICE SOUP WITH LIME

Because there is no recipe more associated with care and affection than chicken soup, the following all-American variety is essential to every collection. We prefer it with rice; however, noodles or barley are good too.

Hints:
1. Boil the chicken a day ahead to remove much of the fat from broth.
2. Slightly over-season broth before adding vegetables for an awesome blend of flavors.

> 1 whole chicken, boiled, skin and bones removed
> 9 cups clear chicken broth
> 1½ cups short-grained white rice, uncooked
> 1 large white onion, chopped
> 1 cup celery, chopped
> 1 cup carrots, shredded
> ¼ cup parsley, chopped
> 1½ tablespoons ground cinnamon
> 1 clove garlic, minced
> 1 tablespoon salted butter
> salt and pepper to taste
> 2 tablespoons fresh lime juice
> lime slices for garnish (optional)

Set aside lime juice and slices. Cube chicken and set aside. In a large saucepan with a tight lid, bring broth to a gentle boil. Add spices, butter, and vegetables. Cover and simmer for 10 minutes or until cinnamon and butter are dissolved. Taste broth to be certain it is rich. If not to your satisfaction, add another tablespoon of salted butter. Add chicken and uncooked rice. Simmer for approximately 25 minutes or until vegetables and rice are cooked to your liking. Stir in lime juice just before serving with toast of choice. Garnish with lime slices if desired.

Yield: 10 servings.

BASIC LEMON EGG SOUP

The taste of lemon juice, chicken flavor and rice combine so well together that many mixtures are produced from it. Greek cuisines rely upon it heavily for many fine dishes.

> 4 cups chicken stock
> 1 large egg
> 1½ tablespoons fresh lemon juice
> ¼ cup rice, uncooked
> salt and pepper

Bring the chicken stock to boil in a large kettle. Once boiling, slowly stir in the rice and allow it to simmer on low heat until cooked, approximately 15 minutes. Beat the egg white until it is stiff; beat the yolk only slightly. Slowly fold the egg yolk into the beaten egg white and stir in the lemon juice. Slowly pour a small portion of the hot chicken stock into the lemon and egg mixture stirring it vigorously. Then pour the thickened egg mixture very slowly into the hot chicken stock stirring constantly. Salt and pepper to taste.
Yield: 6 servings.

CHILLED STRAWBERRY SOUP

As appealing to the eye as to the palate. A sure crowd-pleaser.

> 1 quart fresh strawberries
> 1 cup orange juice
> ⅛ teaspoon ground cinnamon
> 1½ quick-cooking tapioca
> 1 cup buttermilk
> ½ cup sugar
> 2 teaspoons lemon juice
> 1 teaspoon grated lemon peel
> whipped cream or yogurt and fresh mint (optional)

In a blender, combine strawberries, orange juice and cinnamon; cover and process until smooth. Transfer to medium saucepan; add tapioca and let stand for 5 minutes. Bring to a boil and stir for 2 minutes. Remove from the heat; stir in buttermilk, sugar, lemon juice and peel. Refrigerate. Garnish with whipped cream or yogurt and mint. Serve with plate of cinnamon/graham crackers.
Yield: 4 servings.

SPINACH SOUP WITH WHEAT BALLS & LEMON

If you enjoy hearty with a Middle Eastern flair, this one's for you.

　　16 ounces fresh spinach, washed and chopped
　　3 carrots, sliced
　　½ cup dry lentils
　　5 cups water
　　1 medium onion, diced
　　½ teaspoon marjoram
　　1 teaspoon dried mint
　　½ cup lemon juice
　　1 large garlic clove, crushed
　　salt and pepper to taste

Combine all ingredients and heat to boiling. Reduce heat, cover and simmer for 30 minutes.

Wheat Balls:

Margie's hint: To prevent balls from falling apart during cooking, refrigerate for one hour before dropping into hot soup.

　　1 cup fine wheat, washed
　　¼ cup flour
　　¼ teaspoon marjoram
　　¼ teaspoon dried mint
　　salt and pepper to taste

Combine ingredients and knead until sticky. Form into marble size balls. Drop into simmering soup. Cook for an additional 20 minutes. Serve with toasted, garlic pita.
Yield: 6 servings.

GRAPEFRUIT YOGURT SOUP

A deliciously impressive start to any meal and simple to prepare.

　　6 egg yolks
　　¼ teaspoon sugar
　　1 quart plain yogurt
　　6 tablespoons frozen grapefruit juice, thawed and undiluted

Beat egg yolks and sugar until thick and lemon colored. Gently stir in yogurt and grapefruit juice concentrate. Chill. Serve in glass cups or bowls, garnished with mint sprigs for ultimate presentation.
Yield: 4 servings.

CRANBERRY-APPLE-TANGERINE SOUP

A naturally sweet mixture of fruits and juices topped with snappy walnuts. For a healthy variation, substitute honey for white sugar.

2 fresh tangerines, peeled and sectioned
2 apples, peeled, cored, and cut into sections
4 cups cranberries
½ cup uncut walnuts
1 cup white sugar

Remove all of the seeds from the tangerine sections and place them in a food processor or blender along with the apples, cranberries, and sugar. Blend the mixture until it is chopped coarsely, then place it in a container in the refrigerator until good and cold. When you're ready to serve, stir the mixture well, pour it into individual serving bowls and top with walnut halves. Serve cold.
Yield: 3 servings.

EASY BORSCHT WITH LEMON

You don't have to be Russian or Polish to appreciate the flavor of beet soup. Whether served hot or cold, try it tweaked by enough lemon to notice. In Florida we prefer it chilled, but do try it both ways. Talk about the best of two worlds!

Hint: If you try it hot, offer the sour cream as an option and ladle the soup around a boiled potato. Sprinkle with chopped green onion just before serving.

1½ pounds canned beets, reserve liquid
1 10½-ounce can of beef broth
¼ small head green cabbage, shredded
1 small onion, diced
1 stalk celery, diced
3 tablespoons fresh lemon juice
dash each salt and black pepper
sour cream

Purée beets and liquid in a blender. Set aside lemon juice and sour cream. In large sauce pan, add puréed beets to all other ingredients. Simmer until vegetables are cooked. Stir in lemon juice just before serving. Top with sour cream.
Yield: 6 servings.

TANGY MANGO SOUP

We grew up in south Florida where mangos were so prolific neighbors gave them away by the bag. As the population increased so did the popularity of this delicacy, which they now sell in grocery stores. They may be served in any form from appetizer to dessert and with any meal, breakfast to dinner. If you love mangos, try this refreshing cold soup.

> 1 cup fresh orange juice
> 2 large ripe mangos, peeled and sliced
> 1 cup sour cream
> 2 teaspoons fresh lime juice
> ⅓ cup dried apricots

In a medium saucepan combine the dried apricots and fresh orange juice; simmer the mixture over low heat until the apricots become soft and are cooked through, approximately 15-20 minutes. Pour the mixture into a food processor or blender, add the sliced mangos and lime juice and chop until thoroughly blended. Pour the liquid mixture into a bowl and allow it to cool. Once cooled, fold in the sour cream slowly, stirring constantly until it is well blended. Place the mixture into the refrigerator covered and allow it to chill before serving. Serve with rice cakes.
Yield: 4 servings.

CITRUS FROZEN-BOWL SOUP

Picture a hot tropical day, pool-side. The sun is toasting your guests and another cold beverage will cause them to burst. What to do? Serve the following cold soup and be heralded as the hostess "magnifique" and watch them vie for clean-up.

> 2 small melons of choice, halved
> ¼ cup fresh lime juice
> ½ cup fresh orange juice
> 1 cup heavy cream, whipped
> ¼ cup granulated sugar
> 1 lime, thinly sliced
> 4 cinnamon sticks
> 4 sprigs of mint, lemon or spearmint

Wash and slice melons in half. Scoop out seeds and discard. Carefully scoop out flesh to blender pitcher. Do not pierce shells. Place melon shells in freezer, to serve as bowls later. Set aside lime slices and cinnamon sticks. Pulse melon pulp, adding ingredients singly until smoothly blended. Cover and refrigerate until ready to serve. Present in frozen bowls, garnished with lime slices, mint, and a cinnamon stick.
Yield: 4 servings.

SPANISH GAZPACHO

In warm climates the cool spicy taste of gazpacho opens any meal with a clean and eager palate.

    1 large white grapefruit
    1 large pink grapefruit
    3 large oranges
    ¼ cup lime juice
    1 cup ripe avocado, cut in chunks
    1 cup chopped plum tomatoes
    ¼ cup each chopped green bell pepper and seedless
        cucumber
    2 tablespoons chopped red onion
    2 tablespoons chopped fresh cilantro
    2 cloves garlic, minced
    2 chopped green onions
    ½ cup low-sodium vegetable juice
    ½ cup low-sodium tomato juice
    ¼ cup clear chicken broth
    1 teaspoon hot sauce

Pour lime juice over avocado chunks, cover and chill in refrigerator until serving time. This will prevent browning and provide time for the tartness to penetrate. Peel, section and seed grapefruit and oranges. Coarsely chop sections into a large bowl. Add all remaining ingredients, cover tightly and chill 3 hours. At serving time, spoon lime/avocado mixture into individual bowls of gazpacho—do not mix. Garnish bowl rim and soup with fresh cilantro sprigs.
Yield: 4 cups.

LINSENSUPPE
(GERMAN LEMON-LENTIL SOUP)

This hearty soup is made with the ham bone after the cooked shank has provided the family with a grand ham dinner. And what a leftover meal it will be. Partial as we are to beans in any form, soups are a way to stretch the financial and health budgets. We especially enjoy this dish because of the two flavors exuded by the cooked lemon and the juice added at the end. Lusciously different!

16 ounces dry lentils
¼ pound bacon, diced
2 medium onions, sliced
2 medium carrots, diced
2 quarts water
1 cup celery, sliced
3 teaspoons salt or 3 crystals sea salt
½ teaspoons cayenne pepper
½ teaspoon dried thyme
1 large potato, peeled and grated
1 ham bone
2 tablespoons lemon juice
1 large lemon, quartered

Set aside lemon juice. Wash lentils, cover with cold water, and soak overnight. Drain the next day.

In large Dutch oven or soup pot, sauté and brown bacon. Add onions and carrots, and sauté until onions are golden.

Add water and all remaining ingredients with the exception of the juice. Cover and simmer for approximately 3 hours or until lentils are tender. Remove ham bone and trim all meat from it. Discard bone and return meat to the kettle. Remove four lemon wedges and add lemon juice just before serving, whether immediately or the next day. A basket of crusty bread makes a lovely companion.

Yield: 8 servings.

RASPBERRY/CRANBERRY SOUP

Served hot or chilled, raspberry/cranberry soup is as intriguing to doubters as it is beautiful. Try it both ways—you're in for a heavenly surprise. Though fresh may be used in season, utilizing frozen berries works, making it a choice year-round.

> 1 cup frozen raspberries, thawed
> 2 cups frozen cranberries, thawed
> 2 cups apple juice
> ¾ cup sugar
> 2 tablespoons lemon juice
> ¼ teaspoon ground allspice
> 2 cups half-and-half cream, divided
> 1 tablespoon cornstarch
> whipped cream and sprigs of lemon balm or spearmint

In a medium saucepan, bring cranberries and apple juice to a boil. Simmer uncovered for 10 minutes. Press through a sieve and return to pan. Press raspberries through the sieve, discarding seeds and skins. Add to cranberry mixture and bring to boil. Add sugar, lemon juice and allspice; remove from heat. Cool 5 minutes. Stir 1 cup into 1½ cups cream. Return all to pan; bring to a gentle boil. Mix cornstarch with remaining cream; stir into soup. Cook and stir for 2 minutes. Serve hot or chilled. Garnish with whipped cream and lemon balm or spearmint.
Yield: 4 servings.

VEGETABLES & SALADS

SURF & CITRUS SALAD

Travel to Rome for dinner without leaving your kitchen.

> 3 tablespoons fresh lemon juice
> 1 teaspoon honey mustard
> ¼ teaspoon cream style horseradish
> ½ cup olive oil combined with ¼ cup canola oil
> 4 tablespoons locatelli, freshly grated
> ¼ cup red raisins
> ¼ cup whole roasted almonds
> 1 pound steamed, cleaned and shelled shrimp
> 1 scallion, sliced
> 2 large grapefruit, sectioned with seeds and pith removed
> 1½ cups endive pieces, washed and dried
> 1 cup small arugula leaves, washed and dried
> 6 fresh spinach leaves, washed, dried and quartered

On each of four large plates, alternate shrimp and grapefruit sections in equal portions around perimeter of plate, leaving the center for the salad. Layer the greens, raisins and almonds in a large bowl. **Dressing:** Whisk together lemon juice, horseradish and honey mustard. Slowly whisk in the combined oils and season to taste with salt and freshly ground pepper. Pour dressing over greens and gently toss. Heap greens in the center of each plate in equal amounts. Sprinkle with coarsely grated Locatelli just before serving. A basket of Italian bread sliced in generous thickness makes an appropriate aside. **Yield: 4 servings.**

ORANGE SWEET POTATO ROUNDS

Wake up any meal with these brightly colored slices of sweet potato coated with brown sugar and orange rind.

2½ cups sliced boiled sweet potatoes
3 tablespoons butter
3 tablespoons light brown sugar
1 tablespoon grated orange rind
2 tablespoons orange juice

Scrub the sweet potatoes under cold running water and remove any imperfections. Boil them until they can be easily pierced, approximately 20 minutes. Remove the potatoes from the water, peel them, and slice them into approximately ¼-inch thick pieces. Place the disks in a large skillet and sauté them in butter until they are browned on one side. Turn them over and sprinkle the tops with orange juice, sugar, and orange rind. Allow other side to brown slowly on low heat. Be creative in presentation, stack them on plates like pancakes or top your best meat dishes with them.
Yield: 5 servings.

LEMON BROCCOLI

Steaming vegetables retains color and natural flavor like no other method. For this reason, the following dish, though simple to prepare, presents like a platter of nutrients.

1½ pounds of fresh broccoli spears
2 tablespoons lemon rind, finely grated
¼ teaspoon salt
¼ teaspoon black pepper, freshly ground
¼ cup lemon juice
2 cloves garlic, minced
2 tablespoons olive oil
1 lemon, sliced

Steam broccoli spears for 5 minutes or until tender. Combine lemon rind, salt, pepper and garlic. Arrange cooled spears on serving platter and sprinkle with rind mixture and lemon. Garnish with lemon slices, cover with plastic wrap and refrigerate. Serve well chilled.
Yield: 6 servings.

TURKISH VEGETABLES WITH PARSLEY & SESAME OIL

In Middle East food preparation, sesame oil is used extensively in many dishes from salads to dips. Its unique flavor blends well with many foods and especially well with vegetables.

1 cup sesame oil
3 garlic cloves, crushed
1 cup lemon juice
1 teaspoon salt
½ cup water
1½ cups chopped parsley
assorted fresh vegetables

In a small mixing bowl, crush the garlic cloves and mix in a small amount of lemon juice and salt. Stir the mixture well until a smooth paste results. Stir in and mix well the sesame oil, water, and lemon juice and keep stirring until a thick cream forms. Add the parsley and stir the mixture well. Place the sauce into the refrigerator and allow it to chill before serving. Serve in a bowl with cut fresh vegetables.

BLUSHING SPINACH SALAD

Modest yet elegant, this simple salad uses unusual combinations to advantage and illustrates when a drizzle works better than a toss.

1 lemon, thinly sliced and twisted
3 tablespoons lemon juice
¼ cup sugar
6 tablespoons vegetable oil
10 ounces fresh spinach
2 cups sliced fresh strawberries

Combine lemon juice and sugar in a blender. With blender on low, add oil in a slow stream; process until slightly thickened. Just before serving, arrange spinach and strawberries on individual plates; drizzle with dressing. Use lemon twist for garnish and serve with sesame crackers.
Yield: 6 servings.

ORANGE SLAW

Cabbage salad has been served in America for so many years that we think of it as traditionally American. The following preserves the crispness of raw cabbage while blending the sweetness of citrus with the tang of cheese. Deliciously different!

2 cups chopped cabbage
2 carrots, grated
1 small red onion, chopped
2 celery stalks, chopped with leaves
⅓ cup buttermilk
4 ounces crumbled blue cheese
⅓ cup fresh orange juice with pulp
1 cup orange sections
1 tablespoon orange rind, finely grated
1 tablespoon chopped parsley

Set orange sections aside. In large bowl with tight lid, mix all other ingredients. Add orange sections just before serving and toss, gently.
Yield: 4 servings.

MARINATED ARTICHOKE HEARTS WITH LIME

This is such a favorite with the men, you'd be advised to at least double the recipe. The simplicity of it will make you almost ashamed to take a bow—ALMOST.

1 6-ounce jar marinated artichoke hearts, undrained
1 cup sliced mushrooms
¼ cup diced celery
15 ounces cooked black beans
1 lime, sliced and quartered
juice of 1 lime, with pulp
1 tablespoon seasoned-rice vinegar
pinch each granulated garlic, salt and pepper
1 clove garlic, minced

Combine all ingredients in a bowl with a tight lid or use a zip-lock plastic bag. Toss frequently and chill in refrigerator overnight. Toss before serving.
Yield: 4 servings.

NORDIC WATERCRESS-LEMON SALAD

Especially elegant with Alaskan crab cakes but suitable for shrimp, white fish or lobster cakes as well.

    1 bundle fresh watercress, stemmed and chopped
    1 green onion, minced
    2 tablespoons lemon juice, with pulp
    1 large lemon, sliced in rings and seeded
    1 cup light or homemade mayonnaise
    ⅛ teaspoon red pepper, finely ground
    ½ cup whipping cream, whipped

Combine all ingredients and cover. Chill well before serving. Garnish plate with lemon slices and lemon mint or balm. Serve with a basket of crusty bread.
Yield: 2 cups

SALATHA BUTINJAN
(Eggplant Salad)

A popular salad in Middle-Eastern cultures worldwide, Eggplant Salad is usually served at the hottest time of year with ice-cold beverages. An ideal change of pace for south Florida and surprisingly popular with those who will eat eggplant no other way—like Marlene.

Hint: Choose small eggplants to avoid large seeds.

    3 small eggplants, pierced and baked thoroughly
    2 ripe tomatoes, chopped
    ½ cup fresh lemon juice
    3 tablespoons olive oil
    2 tablespoons parsley, chopped
    1 tablespoon basil, chopped
    3 cloves garlic, crushed
    salt and pepper to taste

Preheat oven to 350°. Bake eggplant for 45 minutes or until done. Remove from oven and cool. Peel and mash cooled eggplant. Mix all other ingredients in large bowl. Combine with eggplant, cover and chill at least 1 hour before serving. Serve with garlic chips or pita bread.
Yield: 6 servings.

BASIC BEAN SALAD WITH LEMON

No arsenal of salad recipes would be complete without the diverse multi-bean salad. We make ours the day before, to allow flavors to permeate AND, of course, we use citrus and our favorite beans. Our standard is to use at least four types of beans. We provide a side of grated Parmesan cheese for those who desire a sprinkle.

> 1 15.5-ounce can of each type of beans (garbanzo, black,
>   kidney, light and dark varieties)
> 1 14.5-ounce can of cut or French style green beans
> 3 green onions, coarsely chopped
> ¼ cup shredded carrots
> ½ chopped celery
> 1 clove garlic, crushed
> ½ cup salad oil
> ½ cup seasoned-rice vinegar
> ½ cup lemon juice
> 1 lemon, halved lengthwise and sliced
> 1 lime, halved lengthwise and sliced
> ¼ cup minced green pepper (optional)
> ¼ teaspoon crushed red pepper (optional)
> dash each salt and ground black pepper
> 10 ounces fresh spinach, washed and chopped

Set aside spinach. Cut lemon and lime lengthwise, discard ends and slice. Set aside. Drain all beans and rinse thoroughly. Place together with remaining ingredients in large container with tight lid. Flip several times to gently mix and coat beans with dressing. Toss when you think of it, and refrigerate overnight. The next day, give final tosses before presenting in a deep platter over a bed of chopped, fresh spinach. Garnish with alternating slices of lemon and lime.
Yield: 10 servings.

ORANGE-GLAZED CARROTS

Make it sweet and they'll eat! A sneaky way to get kids to enjoy an important vegetable.

    ¼ cup butter
    ½ cup orange juice
    10 medium carrots, sliced, cooked crisp-tender
    ¼ teaspoon salt
    ¼ tablespoon light brown sugar
    1 tablespoon granulated sugar
    ¼ cup seasoned bread crumbs
    1 tablespoon finely grated orange peel
    6 whole cloves in spice bag of cheese cloth
    chopped parsley

Combine butter, orange juice, sugars, cloves and salt in saucepan. Heat until butter and sugars are melted, mashing any lumps until sauce is hot. Discard spice bag and, in baking dish coated with nonstick spray, pour mixture over drained carrots. Combine peel and bread crumbs; sprinkle over top of carrot mixture and bake in preheated 350° oven for 12 minutes or until top is golden. Sprinkle with parsley before serving.
Yield: 6 servings.

BEETS À L'ORANGE

Because kids concentrate on the flavor and disregard the abundant nutritional value, parents love this combination. Once you try it, canned beets will seem ho hum.

    8 small, fresh beets
    juice of 2 oranges
    1 teaspoon finely grated orange peel
    2 tablespoons orange blossom honey
    1 tablespoon butter
    dash salt

Wash, peel and chop beets finely, approximately 3 cups. Add water to orange juice increasing liquid to 1¼ cups. Combine with beets in saucepan, stir in remaining ingredients, cover and bring to boil. Simmer until beets are desired tenderness, about 15 minutes.
Yield: 4 servings.

BEETS À L'ORANGE 2

Few things are better than the combined sweetness of fruit and vegetables. The taste is an example of Mother Nature at her best and the color doesn't hurt either.

2 large oranges, pulp only
1 tablespoon sweet butter
2 tablespoons brown sugar
1 teaspoon cornstarch
¼ teaspoon orange rind, finely grated
dash each salt and white pepper
2½ cups sliced beets, cooked

Boil sliced beets until tender. In blender, pulse all remaining ingredients for a few seconds. Pour mixture from blender into top portion of a double boiler and heat over water for approximately 10 minutes. Stir sauce regularly. Drain liquid from beets and add cooked beets to orange sauce. Serve with corn bread.
Yield: 8 servings.

POULET DE SOLEIL

The varied textures in this combination make a dazzling presentation of an old chicken salad favorite.

2 cups chopped cooked chicken
1 cup chopped celery
1 cup seedless grapes, halved
½ cup chopped almonds, toasted
1 tablespoon butter
1 11-ounce can mandarin oranges, drained
½ cup mayonnaise
1 teaspoon grated onion
¼ teaspoon salt (optional)
spinach leaves

Melt the butter and toast almonds in small sauté pan. Toss chicken, celery, grapes, orange and almonds in a large bowl. Combine mayonnaise, onion and salt. Gently stir into chicken mixture until all parts are coated. Spoon onto spinach leaves.
Yield: 4 cups.

AUNT MARLENE'S FRUIT SALAD SUPREME

A special tradition in our family because the children can participate in its preparation: the youngest pulls grapes from stems, etc. Our style is to cut the fruit in chunks rather than using a baller concluding that the irregular shapes add to the overall beauty of the salad. Though melon-carved boats have their place, we opt for the largest kettle in the house to make enough for our eager clan.

Hints:
1. Preservatives are unnecessary if you start with citrus and its juices, making sure that all cuts that may turn black on exposure to air are saturated with citrus juice.
2. Adding bananas, watermelon, and delicate berries just before serving will avoid excessive water and permit bananas and berries to retain firmness.
3. Select any ten fruits and you have the idea: use more than that (fresh only!) and you've created a masterpiece.

    ½ cup fresh lime juice
    ¼ cup fresh lemon juice
    6 large grapefruit, sections and juice
    8 large oranges, sections and juice
    1 ripe cantaloupe melon, cut in chunks
    1 honeydew melon, cut in chunks
    2 pounds each red and green seedless grapes
    6 firm bananas, sliced
    1 quart each blueberries and strawberries
        (hulled)
    1 pint each blackberries and raspberries
    4 ripe Bartlett pears, cut in chunks
    1 pint large, sweet cherries, pitted and halved
    4 large, freestone peaches, cut in chunks
    ½ small watermelon, cut in chunks, seeds removed

Place citrus sections and juices in large container. Set aside watermelon chunks in a sealed container. Berries may be combined and set aside in another sealed container. (Bananas are sliced just before serving.) Add remaining fruit to citrus mixture, stirring gently to avoid bruising and making sure to saturate all cuts with citrus juice. Chill in refrigerator for a minimum of 30 minutes.

Add berries to mixture and sliced bananas, making certain to expose slices well to citrus juices. Drain watermelon and remove any seeds missed in preparation, add to salad and stir gently to mix. Serve immediately.
Yield: 12 servings.

CARACAS TINGLE SALAD

The sweetness of citrus mingled with that of red onion provides a flavor unique to the mountainous regions of northern Venezuela. Colorful on the plate as well, a drizzle of dressing permits the distinctive flavors to dominate. Nice change of pace.

⅓ cup olive oil
¼ cup orange juice
3 tablespoons white vinegar
1 garlic clove, minced
1 teaspoon minced fresh parsley
¼ teaspoon salt
dash pepper
8 cups mixed greens
3 oranges, peeled and sliced
1 cup red onions, sliced into rings
½ cup crumbled Gorgonzola cheese
¼ cup slivered almonds, toasted
1 tablespoon butter

Dressing: Whisk together oil, juice, vinegar, garlic, parsley, salt, and pepper.

Melt butter in small sauté pan and toast almonds until golden. Distribute attractively, on individual plates the greens, oranges and onion rings. Drizzle with dressing and sprinkle cheese and almonds atop.
Yield: 8 servings.

GRAPEFRUIT SALAD

It's recipes like this that separate the cooks from the chefs—don't be afraid to try it. You'll surprise yourself.

- 2 large pink grapefruit
- ¼ cup olive oil
- 2 tablespoons red wine vinegar
- 1 teaspoon fennel seed
- ½ teaspoon salt
- ½ pound radish
- 2 green onions, chopped
- 1 large garlic clove, peeled
- 1 tablespoon sunflower seeds, raw or toasted
- 2 tablespoon red raisins

Peel grapefruit and discard all skin and membranes. Break flesh into chunks. Combine oil, vinegar, fennel, and salt. Cover tightly and chill. Grate or shred the radish and combine with the green onions and grapefruit. Chill separately. Just before serving, rub wooden salad bowl with sliced garlic clove so that garlic oil smears onto the bowl's surface. Add grapefruit mixture, sprinkle dressing and toss. Sprinkle individual servings with equal portions of sunflower seeds and red raisins. Serve immediately with chunks of dark bread.
Yield: 4 servings.

STUFFED DATE SALAD

Quick and simple to prepare, this uncommonly delicious dish is extremely popular in the Middle East. Local custom there believes that when the dates are laid out in the shape of a pyramid, the guest will be blessed with eternal life.

Hint: If children are among your guests, try stuffing their dates with crunchy peanut butter sprinkled with confectioners sugar atop. A sure hit!

- 20 pitted dates
- 1 small bag walnut halves
- 1 fresh lemon
- 4 5- or 6-inch perfect, fresh spinach leaves
- 2 tablespoons plain cream cheese

Thoroughly wash spinach leaves and pat dry with a paper towel. Place one spinach leaf on an individual serving plate. Slice the dates halfway thru to the center lengthwise and peel open. Place ⅓ teaspoon of cream cheese in each date, top the cream cheese with a walnut half then fold the date closed. Distribute 5 stuffed dates per serving, arranging them attractively in a fan shape, or circle on the spinach leaf. Drizzle each with a few drops of fresh lemon juice. If desired garnish with a lemon wedge. Serve cold.
Yield: 4 servings.

SUFSOOF
(Tossed Salad with Wheat and Lemon)

Of all the salads of the Middle East, Sufsoof is the most American-like and one of the most requested at our home. Traditionally it is made with iceberg lettuce; however, my family prefers romaine mixed in. An eye-pleaser as well as a healthy combination of fresh vegetables sprinkled with wheat, it is enhanced by the tartness of fresh lemon. Make plenty, as most guests will be looking for seconds.

    1 head iceberg lettuce, washed, dried and diced
    1 head romaine lettuce, washed, dried and diced
    1 cucumber, seeded and chopped
    ½ cup celery, finely chopped
    3 vine-ripened tomatoes, chopped
    3 green onions, sliced
    ½ cup fine wheat
    ¼ cup fresh parsley, diced
    ¼ cup fresh spearmint, diced
    2 tablespoons salt
    2 tablespoons, black pepper, freshly ground
    1 cup olive oil
    1 cup fresh lemon juice
    ¼ cup Calamata olives (optional)

Rinse wheat, drain and cover with lemon juice. Set aside to swell and soften as it absorbs lemon. Place all vegetables in large salad bowl. Pour olive oil over and add olives, herbs, spices and wheat, with whatever lemon has not been absorbed. Toss gently, mixing vegetables and coating all surfaces with dressing. Serve with wedges of warm pita bread.
Yield: 8 servings.

ARABIAN ORANGE, ONION & BLACK OLIVE SALAD

Arabic food preparation characteristically calls for very fresh ingredients, and the bright contrasting colors make this dish as appetizing to the eye as it is to the palate.

> 4 fresh oranges, peeled
> ¼ cup sliced black olives
> 1 medium onion (sweet), cut into rings

> **Dressing:**
> 6 tablespoons olive oil
> juice of ½ lemon
> 1 tablespoon chopped fresh mint
> 1 tablespoon chopped pine nuts
> 1 tablespoon chopped golden raisins or dates
> salt
> freshly ground black pepper

Combine the oil, lemon juice, mint, nuts, raisins, salt and pepper in a small mixing bowl and blend the mixture well. Cut the oranges into thin slices and remove the seeds and bitter white pith. Arrange the orange slices attractively on a serving plate and top with onion rings and sliced olives. Spoon the dressing over the top and add salt and pepper to taste. Serve with basket of muffins.
Yield: 4 servings.

ORANGE SHRIMP SALAD

A company-pleasing presentation and family treat, all in one. If you love shrimp, the following will soon join your repertoire. Satsuma orange sections may be substituted for Mandarin.

> 2 pounds raw medium shrimp, shelled and deveined
> 1 lemon, quartered
> 2 tablespoons chopped fresh parsley
> 24 ounces beer
> 8 ounces drained Mandarin oranges

Steam shrimp with lemon quarters in beer and enough water to cover shrimp. Steam until shrimp turns pink, approximately 3 minutes. Drain and spray cold tap water over shrimp. Drain well.

Honey Mustard Dressing:

½ cup Dijon-style mustard
⅓ cup honey of choice
1 clove garlic, crushed

Whisk ingredients in large bowl. Add mandarin oranges and shrimp sprinkled with parsley—toss. Refrigerate for 1 hour. Toss again before serving on bed of chopped fresh spinach. Serve with a basket of toasted bagel chips.
Yield: 4 servings.

ORANGE & DATE SALAD

Instead of boring guests with a common tossed salad, dazzle them with this vibrant and healthy mixture of fresh fruit, nuts and greens.

1 head romaine lettuce
2 tablespoons chopped walnuts
3 tablespoons chopped dates
36 segments medium fresh oranges
11 ounces of pitted black olives, drained
assorted salad dressings

Pick out 6 perfect lettuce leaves, wash them well and pat them dry with a paper towel. On each serving plate (6 in all) lay out one perfect leaf, bright side up. Remove all of the seeds from the orange segments then arrange approximately 6 orange segments onto each romaine leaf in a star-burst pattern. Combine the walnuts and dates and pile a scoop of the mixture onto the center of the star-burst. Serve cold with salad dressings, permitting your guests to drizzle their choice. Circulate a basket of assorted sweet muffins and dish of pitted black olives.
Yield: 6 servings.

VATICAN CITY SUNSET SALAD

The merits and pungent flavor of rosemary are often ignored by home-makers. Add it to your arsenal of herbs and appear the virtuoso. Experience fresh Mediterranean breezes while enjoying this on your patio.

⅓ cup olive oil
2 tablespoons orange juice
4 tablespoons red wine vinegar
dash each salt and black pepper
1 small red onion
4 large oranges, peeled and sectioned
1 tablespoon minced fresh rosemary
1 head romaine lettuce, torn

Whisk in large serving bowl the oil, orange juice, vinegar, salt, pepper and rosemary. (A teaspoon of dried, crushed rosemary may be substituted for fresh.) Peel and slice onion, dicing slices before adding to mixture in bowl. Gently toss in orange sections and romaine pieces. Serve on chilled, flat plates. Drizzle with dressing and sprinkle with freshly grated Locatelli cheese. Serve with hot Italian bread.
Yield: 8 servings.

ORANGES & AVOCADO SALAD

Watch the faces light up when you present this dish. Oranges like navels, tangelos and honeybells are available in seedless varieties and peel easily making them a natural choice for this dish. Be artistic, use complimentary colored plates and napkins.

1 large ripe avocado
2 large fresh oranges, peeled
½ medium red onion, sliced into rings
1 large head red leaf lettuce
sweet chutney dressing

Wash the lettuce well, and after it has drained of excess water place leaves on a large round serving dish or platter. Peel the oranges, and remove all of the seeds, then separate each orange into individual sections. Arrange the orange sections in the shape of a circle or spiral on the lettuce leaf, starting at the outer edge of the plate and

working toward the center, leaving spaces between them for alternate slices of avocado. Wash a large ripe avocado, then slice it lengthwise around the seed. Rotate the halves to separate them, gently removing the seed with a large spoon. Insert the spoon between the skin and fruit until the skin separates from the fruit. Slice the avocado halves into sections lengthwise making them the same width as the orange sections and arrange them in the spaces between the orange segments. Top the entire salad with rings of sliced red onion and serve cold with the chutney dressing. Your choice of salad dressing can be substituted for the chutney.
Yield: 4 servings.

MANDARIN SALAD GEL

Gelatin salads are as suitable for elegant dinner parties as for casual pool-side luncheons. Try the following combination of crisp veggies sweetened by the Mandarin orange and grapes, all in a bath of cottage cheese.

Hint: Mandarins are convenient but the tangerine is a fine substitute.

  3 ounces orange gelatin
  1 cup hot water
  ¼ cup orange juice, with pulp
  1 tablespoon homemade mayo
  ¼ cup red onion, chopped
  12 green seedless grapes, halved
  ½ cup orange or tangerine sections, well drained
  ½ medium yellow bell pepper, finely chopped
  ¾ cup celery, finely chopped
  8 ounces cottage cheese, small curd, well drained
  ¼ cup green olives, sliced
  1 teaspoon yellow mustard

In 9- by 12-inch glass dish, dissolve gelatin in water. Set aside to cool. Prepare remaining ingredients as required by above list, paying special care to draining of cottage cheese and mandarins. Too much liquid will interfere with gelling process. Stir gelatin to be sure it is thoroughly dissolved. Add remaining ingredients, one at a time, gently stirring to mix and distribute evenly. Refrigerate to set. Cut into squares and arrange on bed of greens before presenting.
Yield: 8 servings.

TRADITIONAL TABBOULEH
(Mint and Parsley Salad)

Because of our Middle Eastern family origin we grew up eating this salad, and rate few dishes better. Raise it a flavor notch by adding chopped fresh tomato. If you like mint add ½ cup mint, chopped fine for that extra special taste.

> 1 cup crushed wheat
> 1½ cups parsley, chopped fine
> 1 cup onions, chopped fine
> ¾ cup olive oil
> 1 cup lemon juice

Clean the crushed wheat in fresh water and soften it by soaking in water for at least 2 hours. Drain and remove any excess water. In a large mixing bowl combine together the onion, parsley, wheat, mint, lemon juice, and oil and blend completely. Season the mixture with salt and pepper. Serve alone or place on a lettuce leaf and garnish if desired with sliced ripe tomato wedges. Serve with pita wedges.
Yield: 4 servings.

LEBANESE CHICKEN TABBOULEH WITH ORANGE

Tabbouleh is famed throughout the world for the zip of lemon flavor it presents. Try it with its sweet sister fruit, the orange, and be treated all over again.

> 1 cup hot chicken broth
> ¾ cup crushed, fine wheat
> 2 teaspoons orange peel, finely shredded
> ¾ cup orange juice
> 2 large oranges, sectioned
> 1½ cups cooked chicken
> 2 tablespoons seeded cucumber
> 2 tablespoons snipped fresh parsley
> 2 tablespoons chopped green onion
> 1 tablespoon snipped fresh mint or 1 teaspoon crushed
>   dried mint

1 tablespoon olive oil
½ teaspoon salt
romaine lettuce leaves

In large mixing bowl pour hot broth and ½ cup orange juice over wheat and let stand a minimum of 30 minutes. Wheat will swell and soften as it absorbs liquid. Cover and chill orange sections and remaining juice. Press wheat to squeeze off excess liquid and stir in peel, remaining juice, chicken, cucumber, parsley, green onion, mint, oil, and salt. Tightly cover and chill 6–8 hours, stirring occasionally. Just before serving, fold in orange sections. Serve on chilled, lettuce-lined plates with a basket of pita bread and bowl of cracked olives.
Yield: 4 servings.

ARABIC SPINACH SAUTÉED WITH PINE NUTS

Spinach and toasted pine nuts together form a perfect partnership. Insure great taste by not overcooking the spinach. Remove the leaves from the water while they still have body and slight crunchiness.

¾ cup green onions chopped fine
2 tablespoons pine nuts
juice from ½ fresh lemon
1 pound fresh spinach
2 tablespoons lite olive oil

Wash the spinach thoroughly and trim away the discolored leaves and rough stems. Blanch the spinach in boiling water quickly (about 30 seconds) then drain it well and chop the leaves into small pieces. Heat the olive oil in a large sauté pan and cook the green onions until they become slightly transparent. Add the pine nuts to the green onions and cook just until the nuts are golden brown. Add the spinach to the mixture and stir for approximately 1–2 minutes being careful to not overcook the spinach. Place the mixture in a serving plate and squeeze fresh lemon juice atop. Serve with warmed pita bread.
Yield: 3 servings.

GREEK CAESAR SALAD

Toasted pita loaves make a nice companion with this salad. Anchovies are not a favorite in our house but may be used to garnish if desired.

¾ cup olive oil
¼ cup lemon juice
1 egg or ¼ cup egg substitute
2 cloves garlic, pressed
1 teaspoon dried oregano
1½ teaspoon salt
⅛ teaspoon pepper
1 head romaine lettuce, torn
¾ cup kalamata olives
1 small purple onion, thinly sliced
½ cup crumbled feta cheese
pita croutons

Using a wire whisk, stir together olive oil, lemon juice, egg, garlic, salt, pepper and oregano. Cover mixture and chill. Toss lettuce, olives, onion and feta in a large bowl. Gradually add enough olive oil to coat leaves, tossing gently. Sprinkle with pita croutons and serve with remaining olive oil mixture.
Yield: 6 servings.

Pita Croutons:
Combine 2 tablespoons olive oil, 1 teaspoon dried oregano, ¼ teaspoon crushed garlic and dash of salt and brush generously over the inside of each pita bread circle. Cut the circles into bite-size pieces and place on a baking sheet. Bake at 400° for 5-7 minutes or until croutons are golden.
Yield: 1⅓ cups.

V

MEATS & SEAFOOD

CURRIED PORK CHOPS WITH CITRUS

Although pork lends itself well to most forms of citrus, our preference is the sweet orange. Try it and then experiment with others for variety. This single recipe will supply you with a storehouse of choices.

  4 center cut, boneless pork chops, well trimmed
      (¾-inch thick)
  1½ cups orange juice
  1½ tablespoons orange blossom honey
  1¼ teaspoons curry powder
  3 oranges, peeled and cut in half-circle slices
  3 tablespoons cornstarch
  ¼ cup water
  2 tablespoon snipped chives

Be sure all separable fat has been removed from the chops then butterfly them. Preheat a large skillet after coating it with nonstick spray. Brown both sides of the chops, draining off excess fat if necessary. Add the orange juice, honey and curry powder, then bring to a boil. Reduce the heat, cover and simmer 35 minutes or until chops are tender and no longer pink. Remove them to a serving platter and keep warm. In the skillet, stir together cornstarch and water. Cook and stir until thickened and bubbly. Time 2 minutes at this state. Stir in orange slices and chives, enough to just heat. Spoon over chops and serve immediately. Rice pilaf and green salad make this ideal for a hearty appetite.
Yield: 4 servings.

FRANK'S ORANGE ROAST PORK

Point the most unlikely man in the direction of a grill or convection oven and he becomes an expert chef—it's magic. Try one of Frank's most requested convection-oven dishes.

> 1 3–4 pound leg of pork, skin removed
> 4 garlic cloves, peeled and halved
> 10 peppercorns
> 2 large white onions
> 3 large oranges, washed and sliced in rounds
> 1 cup dark brown sugar
> 1 cup fresh orange juice, with pulp
> dash each salt, pepper and orange salt (*See* Condiments chapter.)
> ⅓ cup water

Skin and wash the pork under cool running water, then trim away excess fat. With a small paring knife score the roast and insert 8 garlic pieces into slits, distributing evenly. Crush the remaining 8 pieces of garlic with peppercorns and rub mixture over the entire surface of the roast. Sprinkle meat with orange salt. (To make your own, refer to Condiments chapter.) Place on the lower rack of the convection oven and roast at 400° for 45 minutes. Remove meat from oven and discard fat. Return pork to oven, surround with onion halves and pour orange juice with pulp over the roast. Cook for 45 additional minutes or until meat thermometer reflects desired doneness.

Glaze: In a small saucepan prepare glaze of brown sugar and water. Boil until sugar is dissolved and syrup thickens. Transfer cooked onions to serving platter and cover the roast with orange rounds.

Brush the roast and slices with glaze and raise the heat to 450° until the glaze begins to bubble (5–10 minutes).

Remove the roast to a serving platter. Garnish with orange slices.

Serve with Sufsoof (*See* Vegetables & Salads chapter.) and warm pita bread with balls of herb butter.

Yield: 6 servings.

DUCK WITH CRANBERRIES D'ORANGE

The delicate flavor of duck is often missed because of the grease factor. A few simple techniques will enable you to enjoy this speciality. Closely trim fat and skin before cooking, bake on a rack and use a grease mop to remove grease from drippings.

1 2-pound duck, cut in quarters
2 teaspoons arrowroot
2 teaspoons fresh orange juice
orange slices, fresh cranberries and fresh sage leaves
    to garnish

Marinade:
1 cup fresh cranberries
⅔ cup water
2 tablespoons plus 2 teaspoons honey
2 teaspoons fresh orange peel
2 tablespoons fresh orange juice
⅔ cup rosé wine
1 tablespoon plus 1 teaspoon chopped fresh sage leaves
½ teaspoon salt
½ teaspoon black pepper

Trim excess fat and skin from duck. To prepare marinade, in a small saucepan, bring cranberries, water and honey to a boil. Simmer about 10 minutes or until cranberries are tender. Using a wooden spoon, press cranberries through a fine sieve set over a bowl. Stir in the orange peel and juice, wine, sage, salt and pepper. Add the duck to the marinade, turning the duck to coat evenly. Cover and refrigerate for 4 hours or overnight. Preheat oven to 425°. Arrange the duck on a rack in a large baking pan and bake in preheated oven for 45 minutes. Pour the remaining marinade over duck, cover and return to oven. Reduce temperature to 375° and baked for 40 minutes or until the duck is tender. Remove the duck and keep it warm. Blend the arrowroot and orange juice in a small saucepan. Pour off fat or remove with a grease mop. Stir marinade into orange juice. Bring to a boil, stirring constantly, and simmer 1 minute. Pour sauce over duck and garnish with orange slices, cranberries and sage leaves.
Yield: 4 servings.

GERMAN SCHNITZEL

No need to travel to Berlin for this treat when it can be made this easily in your own kitchen. Top the meal off with a Bavarian dessert and you will hear ump-pah-pahs all around the table.

 6 center-cut pork chops, boned
 2 eggs
 3 tablespoons milk
 2 cups bread crumbs
 ½ cup vegetable oil
 juice from 2 lemons
 1 lemon, sliced

Pound chops to ¼-inch thickness. Beat the eggs and milk. Dip the pork chops in the egg mixture, then in the bread crumbs. Repeat process. Fry in 350° oil until golden brown. Place on a serving platter, garnished with lemon slices. Drizzle lemon juice over chops just before serving. Serve with hot potato salad and dark bread. **Yield: 4 servings.**

GARLIC CHICKEN

An accommodating dish equally suitable as the entrée at a formal dinner as when the wings are used for a unique nibble at a Super Bowl party. We've even received rave reviews for it at a bridal shower. The ultimate in the finger-lickin'-good category.

 2 chickens, 2–3 pounds each, cut in pieces and skinned
 2 each lemons and limes, sliced
 1 cup lemon juice
 1 teaspoon each salt and black pepper
 ½ teaspoon granulated garlic
 3 cloves fresh garlic, peeled and sliced
 2 tablespoons chopped parsley
 3 tablespoons dried oregano
 paprika
 1 cup olive oil

Preheat the oven to 350°. Coat a large roasting pan with nonstick spray. Clean and pat the chicken pieces dry. Pour ½ cup olive oil in the pan, turning the pan about to coat the bottom. Arrange the chicken pieces in the pan. Pour the remaining oil and 1 cup of lemon juice over the chicken and sprinkle them with all spices, including sliced garlic.

Reserve the paprika. Chill the citrus slices. Cover loosely with foil and bake for 30 minutes. Remove the foil, and arrange half of each type citrus slices (reserving other half for serving platter garnish) atop chicken pieces and sprinkle with paprika. Baste each piece with lemon oil from pan before returning to oven. Bake uncovered for 20 minutes longer or until chicken is a honey-colored brown.
Yield: 4 servings.

LATINO AMERICANA LIME-CHICKEN

The juice of citrus fruits is commonly used throughout Latin America. It not only gives meat a refreshingly different taste, but the citric acid in it acts as a natural tenderizer.

2 tablespoons fresh lime juice
1 cup medium salsa
3 tablespoons vegetable oil
½ cup medium hot taco sauce
2 chicken breasts, halved, skinned, and boned
½ teaspoon grated lime peel
¼ cup honey
Lime yogurt

In a medium mixing bowl combine the lime juice, honey, salsa, and the lime peel and mix well. Remove about one fourth of the marinade for later then place the chicken breasts in the remaining mixture and allow them to marinate in the refrigerator for at least 1 hour. Remove chicken from the marinade and, in an iron skillet on medium heat, cook the chicken breasts in oil until they are golden brown, approximately 6–8 minutes. Pour the reserved marinade and taco sauce over the chicken breasts and continue cooking on low heat for an additional 10–12 minutes or until chicken is cooked through. Serve the chicken with a dollop of lime yogurt and sprinkle each with chopped fresh parsley.
Yield: 4 servings

Lime Yogurt:
1 teaspoon finely grated lime zest
½ cup yogurt
¼ teaspoon lime juice

Fold together all ingredients in a small mixing bowl.

ITALIAN ONE-POT

A recipe borrowed from an Italian neighbor, this is an oft-visited pot at our Super Bowl buffets. If you have one large enough, use your slow-cooker so the hostess can join the party. We prefer lamb but meat and beans of choice can be used. Be creative and make your own version.

1 cup dried pinto beans
1 cup dried great northern beans
1 cup dried black beans
3 tablespoons olive oil
1 medium yellow onion, diced
6 garlic cloves, diced
2 celery stalks, diced
2 carrots, diced
6 large lamb shanks
8 ounces fresh spinach, washed and coarsely chopped
2 cups clear chicken broth
1½ cups peeled, seeded and chopped plum tomatoes
4 tablespoons tomato paste
dash salt and coarsely ground black pepper
2 tablespoons finely chopped fresh parsley
2 tablespoons finely chopped fresh spearmint
1 tablespoon finely grated lemon peel
1 large lemon, halved, sliced and seeded

Sort and rinse the beans thoroughly. More than cover the beans with water and allow to soak overnight. In a large skillet braise the lamb shanks in oil over medium heat, then remove the shanks to a crock pot. Add the celery, carrots and onion to the skillet and simmer until tender. Add the garlic, stirring constantly and cook for an additional 2 minutes. Pour into the crock pot. Drain the beans, rinse with cold water and add to the pot. Add all remaining ingredients, stir gently, cover and set the pot on the highest temperature for one hour. Stir and reduce to the lowest temperature and cook for six hours or until the beans are tender and the meat is nearly separated from the bone. Place the bowls and ladle adjacent to the pot for self-serving. Place basket of crusty, bread hunks nearby.

Yield: 6 servings.

HUNGARIAN STUFFED CABBAGE (Holishkes)

A mild, sweet-sour flavor reminds us of days past.

Hint: Squeezing holishkes gently after rolling and placing a glass pie plate atop will secure them and eliminate the need to fasten with toothpicks.

 1 green cabbage, large enough to yield 12–14 leaves
 beef bones
 2 onions, chopped
 1 pound ground beef
 1 small onion and 1 tablespoon water, pulverized in blender
 1 28-ounce can peeled and crushed tomatoes
 3 teaspoons salt
 dash each ground cinnamon and black pepper
 ½ cup rice, uncooked
 1 beaten egg
 ¼ cup lemon juice
 3 tablespoons brown sugar
 ¼ cup red raisins (optional)

Core the cabbage and submerge it in a kettle of boiling water. Carefully separate the leaves, removing each to a large baking pan when just pliable. Allow to cool. In a saucepan simmer the bones, tomatoes (reserving 2 tablespoons juice), and chopped onions over medium heat. Mix the reserved juice, raisins, beef, pulverized onion, 1½ teaspoons of salt, pepper, cinnamon, rice and egg. Trim the core from cabbage leaves, set it aside. Place a large walnut-size amount of filling on each leaf and spread lengthwise. Fold tip end over filling and roll, cigar like. Press slightly and trim excess cabbage leaf from open core end. Remove bones from tomato mixture and discard them. Line a stainless steel kettle with core of cabbage and place holishkes side-by-side atop. If a second row is necessary, place them diagonally across the first level. Sprinkle salt and add tomato mixture. Add enough water to cover the holishkes, if necessary. Place a glass pie plate on the holishkes applying slight pressure. Cover with a lid and simmer for 1 hour. Blend the lemon juice with sugar, adding more lemon if needed to thin. Carefully remove glass plate and pour lemon juice mixture over. (Taste sauce and adjust lemon or sugar to taste.) Simmer uncovered for 15 minutes. Serve with warm crusty bread.
Yield: 6 servings.

GERMAN SOUR VEAL WITH NOODLES

Tender veal that's packed with flavor.

    3 pounds boned veal, cut in serving pieces
    1 large onion, peeled
    1 dozen whole cloves
    1 tablespoon flour
    2 cups lemon juice
    salt and pepper
    8 ounces medium noodles
    3 tablespoons butter

Cover the veal pieces with cold water, and add the onion studded with cloves. Cover and simmer for 2 hours or until tender. Drain, and reserve the broth. Remove the onion and trim any fat off the veal. Blend the flour with 1 tablespoon of lemon juice then add it to the broth, stirring constantly. Add the remaining lemon juice to the broth. Simmer stirring as the broth begins to thicken. When at the desired thickness, add generous shakes of salt and pepper. Cook the noodles in a saucepan until tender then drain. Add butter and flip until the butter is melted and coats the noodles. Pour onto 6 individual serving dishes. Spoon veal into center of noodle beds and distribute sauce among four plates. Serve with basket of black bread and fresh banana.
Yield: 6 servings.

*MARINATED FLANK STEAK WITH CITRUS SALSA

A hearty beef dish, with the zest of the Spanish Caribbean. To warm tortillas, stack them and wrap in foil. Heat in a 350° oven for 10 minutes.

    ¾ cup frozen Florida orange juice or
        grapefruit juice concentrate, thawed
    1 or 2 jalapeño peppers, seeded and finely chopped
    1 teaspoon black pepper
    1 teaspoon paprika
    ½ cup water
    1 1- to 1½-pound beef flank steak
    ¼ cup thinly sliced green onions

2 tablespoons snipped parsley
1 tablespoon lime juice
dash salt
2 Florida oranges, peeled, seeded and chopped
1 Florida grapefruit, peeled, seeded and chopped
6 6- to 7-inch flour tortillas, warmed

For garnish (optional):
jalapeño peppers
1 Florida grapefruit, sliced

For marinade, in a small bowl combine thawed orange or grapefruit
juice concentrate, finely chopped jalapeño pepper, black pepper and
paprika. Reserve 2 tablespoons of the mixture of salsa. Add the water
to remaining mixture.

Score steak by making shallow cuts at 1-inch intervals diagonally
across steak in a diamond pattern. Repeat on second side. Place in a
plastic bag set in a shallow dish. Pour marinade over steak; close bag.
Marinate in the refrigerator 2 to 24 hours; turn bag occasionally.

For salsa, in a nonmetallic bowl stir together the 2 tablespoons
juice concentrate mixture, the onions, parsley, lime juice and salt.
Add chopped oranges and grapefruit; stir gently. Cover and chill at
least 30 minutes to blend flavors.

Remove meat from bag. Discard marinade. Place meat on the
grill rack of an uncovered grill. Grill directly over medium coals,
turning once, allowing 12 to 14 minutes for medium-rare.

Thinly slice meat. If desired, garnish with jalapeños and
grapefruit slices. Serve with salsa and warmed tortillas.
Yield: 6 servings.

To Broil: Place steak on the unheated rack of a broiler pan. Broil
3 inches from heat for 6 minutes. Turn and broil 7 to 8 minutes more
for medium-rare. Serve as above.

*FLORIDA FAJITAS

This marinade gives great flavor to the skirt steak. The fajitas are fun and festive to prepare and serve. Goes great with Grapefruit Salsa and Grapefruit Guacamole Salsa.

4 cups Florida grapefruit juice
½ cup vinegar or lime juice
½ to ¾ cup olive oil
½ cup fresh chopped rosemary (⅓ cup dried)
1 large head garlic, mashed
⅓ cup chopped oregano
¼ cup ground cumin
2 tablespoons cayenne
2 tablespoons Worcestershire sauce
1 8-ounce jar mustard
1 onion, minced
1 to 2 cups dry wine as desired
3 pounds skirt steaks

Combine all of the ingredients in a large shallow dish and marinate the meat in the refrigerator for at least one day. Barbecue over hot coals until the meat has reached medium doneness, using the marinade to baste the meat while grilling. Slice the meat thin across the grain and serve with black beans, flour tortillas and Grapefruit Salsa. **Serves 8 to 10.**

*ORANGE TERIYAKI GLAZED CHICKEN WITH CITRUS WILD RICE

2 boneless, skinless chicken breasts (about 1½ pounds)

Marinade Glaze:
1 cup fresh Florida orange juice, plus 3 strips orange zest
1½ cup soy sauce
⅓ cup honey
4 cloves garlic, minced
4 scallions, white part minced, green part thinly sliced for garnish
1 tablespoon minced fresh ginger
1 cinnamon stick
2 teaspoons sesame oil
Citrus Wild Rice (*See* Rice & Pasta chapter.)

Wash and dry the chicken breasts, trimming off any fat or sinew. Cut the breasts into halves and place in a shallow baking dish. Place the orange juice in a saucepan and boil until reduced by half. Add the soy sauce, honey, garlic, scallion whites, ginger, cinnamon stick, and sesame oil. Boil the mixture until thick and syrupy, about 5 minutes. Remove the pan from the heat and strain the glaze into a bowl. Let cool to room temperature. Pour half the mixture over the chicken breasts, turning the breasts to coat both sides. Marinate the chicken breasts in this mixture for 30 minutes.

Just before serving, preheat the grill or broiler to high. Grill the chicken breasts until cooked, 2 to 3 minutes per side, basting with the remaining glaze. Sprinkle the chicken with chopped scallion greens and serve at once with Citrus Wild Rice.

GLAZED RIBS

The sweet combination of citrus juices and marmalade infuse the meat with real tropical taste.

> 4 pounds spareribs, cut in 3 or 4 rib portions
> 1 teaspoon salt
> 1 cup lime juice
> ½ cup dark corn syrup
> 2 tablespoons each lemon and orange juice
> 2 tablespoons butter
> 1 cup orange marmalade, melted
> ½ teaspoon ground ginger
> 2 cups orange sections, seeded

Preheat the oven to 450°. Place the ribs on the rack of a broiler pan and bake uncovered for 30 minutes. Drain off the excess fat and reduce the heat to 350°. Set aside orange slices. In a saucepan, combine the remaining ingredients and heat. Arrange the drained ribs in a baking dish. Top with orange sections. Place remaining rib portion, crosswise, over the orange sections and pour syrup mixture over all. Cover and bake for 1 hour, basting with syrup mixture every 20 minutes. Uncover and continue baking for 20 minutes or until the ribs are tender and glazed.
Yield: 6 servings.

MIDDLE EASTERN ROASTED CHICKEN

Middle Eastern food is known for its subtle flavors and exotic herbs and spices. Try this recipe calling for ingredients found in most kitchens and treat your family to a night at the Casbah.

1 large (4–5 pound) roasting chicken
3 garlic cloves, 2 generously sliced lengthwise, 1 halved
1 tablespoon each salt, black pepper and ground allspice
2 tablespoons olive oil
8 fresh lemon mint or spearmint leaves
¼ cup lemon juice
1 lemon, quartered, seeds removed
1 cup orzo

Clean the chicken under cool running water then pat it dry. Preheat the oven to 350º. Mix the salt, pepper, and allspice with the oil to form a thin paste, then soak half the mint leaves and clove slices, set aside. With fingers, gently insert soaked clove slice and mint leaf under skin of the bird, distributing as evenly as possible. Take caution not to tear the skin; pat each insertion firmly in place. Rub the skin of the bird with the remaining paste. Place the bird breast up on rack in roasting pan that has been sprayed with nonstick spray. Place halved clove with 1 quarter lemon wedge in neck cavity, tuck skin under bird. Tuck wings, insert remaining 3 quarters lemon wedges, garlic slices and mint leaves set aside, in body cavity. Tie crossed drumsticks with twine. Pour 1½ cups chicken broth in the pan and lemon juice over the bird. Cover with aluminum foil and bake for 30 minutes. Remove the foil, baste with pan juices, remove fat with grease mop. Add orzo to the juices, stir and bake for 1 hour or until bird is golden brown and drumsticks begin to separate from body. Carve and serve surrounded by orzo on large platter. Garnish with lemon wedges and mint or parsley sprigs. Serve with basket of pita bread and bowl of tabbouleh.
Yield: 6 servings.

CUBAN CITRUS MARINATED CHICKEN

A delicious and convenient Latin dish for the individual with an appreciation for fine cuisine, a modest budget and little time for kitchen duties.

    4 4-ounce chicken breast halves, boneless,
        skinless
    ½ teaspoon finely grated lime peel
    1 tablespoon fresh lime juice
    1 tablespoon orange blossom honey
    1 tablespoon soy sauce
    ⅓ cup orange juice
    2 teaspoons cornstarch
    2 oranges, peeled and sectioned

Preheat the oven to 350°. Rinse and pat the chicken dry then arrange them in an 8- by 8- by 2-inch baking dish. In a small bowl combine the lime peel, lime juice, honey and soy sauce. Pour mixture over the chicken and tightly cover with foil. Place on the middle shelf in the oven and bake for 20 minutes. Remove the foil and pour the juices through a strainer and into a saucepan.

Sauce: Add orange juice and cornstarch to the reserved juices and simmer for 3–4 minutes stirring constantly until thickened. Distribute the orange sections over the chicken, pour the thickened gravy over the chicken and bake uncovered for an additional 10 minutes to thoroughly cook the chicken and warm the oranges. Transfer to a serving platter, pour the sauce over the chicken and serve with hot buttermilk biscuits and flavored spread of choice.

Yield: 4 servings.

**An outdoor variation we recommend for the above, is to add 2 tablespoons olive oil to lime, honey and soy sauce and marinate chicken breasts in refrigerator for one hour. Add mesquite chips to coals of barbeque and grill chicken until done, but not overcooked. Baste with marinade and remove to serving platter. Spoon over orange sauce as in above before serving.

LEMON CHICKEN WITH WALNUTS

Lemon not only adds flavor and moisture to chicken but it tenderizes it too. Walnuts add crunchiness and a naturally sweet taste. Together they make this dish extraordinary.

>   1 2½- to 3-pound chicken, quartered
>   3 tablespoons butter
>   2 tablespoons chopped scallions
>   1 tablespoon all-purpose flour
>   1 teaspoon ground ginger
>   1½ cups beef stock
>   salt
>   fresh ground pepper
>   1 tablespoon molasses
>   grated peel of 1 lemon
>   2 tablespoons lemon juice
>   ½ cup chopped walnuts

Preheat the oven to 350º. Sprinkle the outside of the chicken with salt and pepper. In a large skillet melt the butter then add the chicken and brown it. Once browned remove the chicken and place it in a large baking tray. Add the onion to the skillet juices and sauté them until they become transparent. Stir in the flour and the ginger and cook for 1 minute while constantly stirring. Stir in the stock slowly and boil for 1 minute. Add the molasses, lemon peel, lemon juice and the chopped walnuts and mix thoroughly then pour the mixture over the chicken. Cover the baking tray with foil and bake for 1 hour or until the chicken is done. When done cooking, garnish the chicken with lemon peel, walnuts, and parsley.
Yield: 4 servings.

ORANGE-ROASTED CORNISH HENS

A reliable pair of kitchen shears makes this impressive dish easy to prepare. To split Cornish game hens in half, simply cut through the breastbone, just off center. Next cut through the center of the backbone. The presentation is elegant when displayed over a bed of wild rice. Better double this recipe as even the most modest of appetites will be looking for second helpings.

1 small onion, finely chopped
1 clove garlic, minced
½ cup chicken broth
2 tablespoons vegetable oil
1 teaspoon finely shredded orange peel
½ cup orange juice
2 tablespoons honey
4 teaspoons cornstarch
3 Cornish game hens, 1½ pounds each, split lengthwise
1 orange, cut into 6 wedges
orange slices and parsley sprigs for garnish

In small saucepan, cook the garlic and onion in oil until onion is tender. Add the chicken broth, orange peel, orange juice, honey, and cornstarch to the onion mixture and, stirring constantly, cook until thickened. Cook for 2 minutes after mixture begins to bubble. Remove from the heat. Clean the hen halves and pat them dry. In a shallow roasting dish sprayed with a nonstick coating, place each hen half atop one orange wedge. Baste each chicken half with a spoonful of the hot citrus marinade. Bake uncovered for 45 minutes at 350º. Baste regularly and bake another 15 minutes. Carefully lift halves to bed of cooked wild rice on serving platter, garnish with orange slices and parsley sprigs.
Yield: 6 servings.

SPICY BAHAMIAN CHICKEN WITH CITRUS SALSA

Bahamian style cooking is sassy, hot and spicy. Here's just one delicious example.

> 6 skinless, boneless chicken breasts, halved and pounded
> 1 cup frozen orange juice concentrate, thawed
> 1 small white onion, cut up
> ½ teaspoon crushed red pepper
> ½ teaspoon ground allspice
> ½ teaspoon curry powder
> 2 each large grapefruit and oranges
> ½ cup mango chutney, cut up
> 2 tablespoons bias-sliced green onions

Chicken: Rinse chicken under cool water then pat dry before pounding. In a blender container, combine thawed concentrate, white onion, red pepper, allspice, curry powder, dash each salt and pepper. Cover and blend until nearly smooth. Place chicken in plastic bag set in shallow dish. Add orange mixture; turn to coat all sides and seal. Chill for 3–6 hours.

Salsa: Peel and section grapefruit and oranges over a dish to catch juices. Discard any seeds and membranes, then coarsely chop the citrus. Add citrus, chutney, and onion to juices in bowl. Cover and chill for 1 hour.

Remove the chicken from marinade, reserving marinade. Place chicken on the unheated rack of a broiler pan and broil 4 inches from heat for 5 minutes. Turn and brush with reserved marinade; discard any remaining. Broil 7–10 minutes more or until chicken is tender and thoroughly cooked. Serve chicken on plate with salsa and slices of Cuban bread.

Yield: 6 servings.

ORANGE-GLAZED CHICKEN ROLLS

Busy schedules do not always permit hours for food preparation. Orange-Glazed Chicken Rolls can be prepared ahead and will taste as though they were slaved over for hours. The recipe even lends itself to other meats and fish. Be creative and enjoy the compliments.

2 medium carrots, peeled
1 medium yellow, red or green pepper, cut into strips
4 medium skinless, boneless chicken breast halves (12-ounce)
1 teaspoon margarine or butter
¼ teaspoon curry powder
¼ cup orange marmalade

Halve the carrots crosswise and cut each piece into 4 sticks and place in ¼ cup of water in a saucepan and simmer covered for 4 minutes, or until crisp-tender. Add the peppers and simmer for an additional 3 minutes then drain and set aside. Rinse the chicken and pat dry then place on plastic wrap and fold over and, with a meat mallet, pound lightly to approximately ¼-inch thickness. Melt margarine or butter and combine with curry powder then brush the mixture on top side of the chicken only, place carrots and peppers crosswise on short end of chicken pieces and roll up. Secure the rolls with wooden toothpicks. Arrange the rolls in a baking dish that has been sprayed with a nonstick spray. Cover with foil and bake in preheated 350° oven for 20 minutes. Remove from oven and pour glaze over the rolls and return them to the oven uncovered for an additional 5 minutes.

Glaze: In a small saucepan heat marmalade on low heat until it is just melted. Spoon over chicken.

Yield: 4 servings.

INDONESIAN LAMB KEBABS

This lamb-on-a-skewer recipe makes any occasion special. For the outdoor afficionados try cooking it on a grill for that added taste and adventure.

1 pound lamb for stew, cut into 1-inch cubes
salt
12 medium mushrooms
½ cup plain yogurt
1 teaspoon ground ginger
1 garlic clove, crushed
¼ teaspoon ground cumin
¼ teaspoon ground coriander
3 tablespoons lemon juice
1 tablespoon vegetable oil
fresh ground pepper
2 medium onions
1 green bell pepper, cleaned and cut into 8 pieces
1 red bell pepper, cleaned and cut into 8 pieces

Combine together in a medium mixing bowl the yogurt, ginger, garlic, cumin, coriander, lemon juice, oil, salt and pepper and stir until thoroughly blended. Add the lamb pieces and stir until the lamb is well coated then cover and allow to marinate in the refrigerator for several hours or, even better, overnight. When ready to prepare, preheat the broiler. Blanch the onions in boiling water for 3 minutes and drain. Once they have cooled, quarter the onions and on wooden skewers alternate an onion quarter, piece of lamb, slices of bell peppers, and a mushroom. Keep placing on skewers until all ingredients have been used up. Place the skewers on a broiler pan and brush with the marinade then cook under the broiler for 15 to 20 minutes. While cooking, baste frequently with the marinade. Serve over cooked rice or alone.
Yield: 4 servings

*CITRUS & MUSHROOM CHICKEN

For casual entertaining, this fast and fantastic dish is a winner. You'll only need to leave your guests for a few minutes to cook the chicken and citrus sauce.

    6 skinless, boneless chicken breast halves (about
        1¼ pound total)
    1½ cups water
    ¾ cup frozen Florida Orange Juice concentrate, thawed
    3 tablespoons balsamic vinegar or white wine vinegar
    2 tablespoons cornstarch
    2 teaspoons instant chicken bouillon granules
    2 tablespoons olive oil
    4 cups sliced shiitake or button mushrooms
    12 ounces refrigerated fresh or packaged dried tomato
        linguine and/or plain linguine, cooked and drained
    Florida orange slices, halved (optional)

Rinse chicken; pat dry with paper towels. Season chicken breasts lightly with salt and pepper. For sauce, in a bowl stir together water, thawed concentrate, vinegar, cornstarch, and bouillon granules; set aside.

In a 12-inch skillet cook chicken in hot oil for 8 to 10 minutes or until tender and no longer pink, turning once. Remove chicken from skillet; cover and keep warm.

In the same skillet cook mushrooms until tender. Stir sauce and add to skillet. Cook and stir until thickened and bubbly. Cook and stir for 2 minutes more. Serve sauce over chicken and hot cooked linguine. If desired, garnish with orange slices.

Makes 6 servings.

JAMAICAN SWEET PORK TENDERLOIN

A delightful scent will emanate from your broiler, bringing outdoor grilling pleasures inside. If using lamb instead of pork, use maple or mint in place of rum. Better yet, try it both ways.

2 pork tenderloins approx. 1 pound each
1 teaspoon cornstarch
dash salt
2 tablespoons dark brown sugar
½ teaspoon ground ginger
1 cup orange juice
1 tablespoon lemon juice
1 teaspoon rum flavoring
8 slices bacon
8 cherry tomatoes
1 medium green pepper, cut into 8 pieces
2 oranges, quartered and seeded

Slice the tenderloin into 1-inch chunks. Mix the sugar, cornstarch, salt and ginger in a small saucepan. Stir in the juices and cook over low heat, stirring constantly until the mixture thickens (2 minutes). DO NOT BRING TO A BOIL. Remove from the heat and stir in the rum flavoring. Thread the tenderloin chunks on four 12-inch skewers, twist bacon slices between the chunks, leaving some room between. Brush with sauce and place skewers on broiler pan rack about 4 inches from broiling element. Broil 5 minutes; turn and baste with sauce. Broil 5 minutes on other side. Add lemon quarters, pepper and tomatoes to each skewer in alternating fashion. Brush with sauce and return to broiler for 4 minutes longer. Turn once after 2 minutes. Serve over bed of saffron rice. Garnish platter with curls of orange rind, thinly peeled.
Yield: 4 servings.

DOLPHIN VERONIQUE

Culinary legend has it that the chef who created the Veronique style, named it after his assistant's newborn daughter. Whatever the source, the name has come to promise the delicate flavors of wine and grapes. Add citrus to the mix and you have impacted a classic. Frank, being quite a fisherman, regularly stocks our freezers with bass, flounder and dolphin. We decided to apply the Veronique style to dolphin with the following result.

Hint: We have found that using a rack eliminates soaking the fillets in liquid and reduces the breakage hazard when transferring to plates. If that is not a problem for you, cook in liquid. It's yummy either way.

4 dolphin fillets
½ cup peanut oil
½ cup white wine
1 teaspoon salt
1 clove garlic, minced
2 teaspoons cornstarch
1 medium onion, minced
⅓ cup orange juice
1 teaspoon lemon butter
1 tablespoon parsley, chopped
2 tablespoons slivered orange peel
1 cup halved seedless white grapes
1 orange, sliced

In a 10" skillet add the onion, oil, and garlic. When the onion is soft, add the wine and orange peel, then stir to blend. Lightly coat the rack with nonstick spray and place in the center of the skillet. Place the fillets on the rack and sprinkle with salt and pepper and dot each with ¼ teaspoon lemon butter. Pour wine and orange juice over, then cover and simmer for 5–10 minutes or until the fillets easily flake with a fork. Lift the rack and fillets out of the skillet. Carefully transfer fillets to plates, garnish with orange slices. Slowly add cornstarch and grapes to the skillet and stir until the gravy thickens slightly. Apply 1 tablespoon sauce to each fillet. Serve remaining sauce in gravy boat so that each guest may add more.
Yield: 4 servings.

THAI HONEY SHRIMP TEMPURA

Thai cooking, long enjoyed in specialty restaurants, can now be experienced at home with this simple, yet elegant meal.

> 8 jumbo shrimp with tails
> oil of choice for deep frying
> 1 teaspoon arrowroot
> tangerine or satsuma wedges and herb sprigs to garnish

Marinade:
> 1 tablespoon light soy sauce
> 1 tablespoon dry sherry
> 2 teaspoons finely grated tangerine or satsuma peel
> 1 tablespoon tangerine or satsuma juice
> 1 garlic clove, crushed
> 2 teaspoons orange blossom honey
> ½ teaspoon black pepper

Batter:
> ¾ cup all-purpose flour
> ¼ teaspoon salt
> ¼ teaspoon dry mustard powder
> ¼ teaspoon black pepper
> 1 tablespoon plus 1 teaspoon olive oil
> ⅓ cup beer
> 2 egg whites

Marinade: In a large bowl, combine all marinade ingredients until well mixed. Add the shrimp, turning in the marinade to coat evenly. Cover and refrigerate for 2 hours.

Batter: In a large bowl, combine flour, salt, dry mustard and pepper. Make a well in the center. Using a wooden spoon, mix in olive oil and beer to form a batter. Beat until smooth. Cover and refrigerate 30 minutes. Drain shrimp well. Whisk egg whites until stiff and fold into batter. Half-fill a deep saucepan with oil. Heat to 350º. Hold the shrimp by the tails and dip into the batter. Fry in oil 2 to 3 minutes or until golden brown. Drain on paper towels and keep warm. Blend arrowroot and marinade in a small saucepan. Bring to boil, stirring constantly. Cool 30 seconds. Arrange 2 shrimp on each serving plate. Spoon a small amount of sauce over shrimp. Garnish with tangerine wedges and fresh herb sprigs.
Yield: 4 servings.

FILLETS FLORENTINE WITH GRAPEFRUIT

What could be better than a melange of a favorite fish, vegetable and fruit? We like flounder for this dish because of its delicate flavor and ease in handling. Experiment with several types, if they don't roll well, layer them, but stick with the spinach and grapefruit. You'll like it.

6 fillets
1 tablespoon minced garlic
1 teaspoon paprika
½ cup fresh parsley, chopped
1 small onion, diced
¼ cup pine nuts
6 ounces spinach, cooked and drained
¾ cup white zinfandel
3 tablespoons butter, sweet
2 teaspoons cornstarch
2 chicken bouillon cubes
2 pink or red grapefruit, sectioned

Rinse and dry the fish fillets. Sprinkle them with paprika, 1 teaspoon parsley and garlic. Sauté the pine nuts and onions in 1 tablespoon of butter. Mix the combination with cooked spinach. Distribute equal amounts of the mixture widthwise on each fillet, at the widest part. Roll the fillet over the spinach filling, and secure with a wooden pick. Arrange the rolled fillets in a baking dish, pour wine over them and marinate in the refrigerator for several hours. Baste or rotate regularly. Transfer the fillets and wine to a heavy skillet, cover and poach. Remove fish rolls to serving platter. Strain liquid into measuring cup. Add water if necessary to make 1 cup liquid. Melt 2 tablespoons butter and blend in cornstarch, stirring until smooth. Add cup of poaching liquid and bouillon cubes and heat to boiling. Stir constantly. Remove from heat. Add grapefruit sections and remaining parsley. Pour over and around fish rolls and serve immediately.
Yield: 6 servings.

SIMPLE & ELEGANT LOBSTER THERMIDOR

Most gourmet dishes can be simplified so they can be prepared with regularity and panache by anyone with desire. Lobster Thermidor is a case in point.

     8 ounces cheddar cheese, chopped or grated
     2 cups milk
     2 cups lobster chunks, cooked
     ½ cup butter
     ½ cup corn starch
     ½ cup lemon juice
     1 tablespoon parsley, dried
     1 lemon, sliced
     sprigs of lemon mint

In the top of a double boiler melt the butter, then add the milk slowly, then the corn starch stirring constantly until thickened. Add the cheese and continue stirring until completely melted. Remove from the heat and stir in the lemon juice and lobster chunks. Cover and let stand for 5 minutes to heat the lobster. Stir in the parsley and pour into individual casserole dishes. Place on metal chargers, garnished with lemon slices and sprigs of mint. Serve immediately with a basket of crackers or toasted dark bread.
Yield: 6 servings.

GREEK BACON-WRAPPED SHRIMP

The flavor enhancing qualities of bacon are extremely versatile for a wide range of foods from salads to meats. On shrimp the moisture and smoky taste combine to create a deliciously unique flavor. To reduce preparation time, use the larger jumbo shrimp.

     20 large shrimp, cleaned, peeled and de-veined
     1 tablespoon oregano powder
     1 tablespoon fresh parsley, minced
     1 tablespoon granulated garlic
     1 tablespoon fresh ground black pepper
     1 teaspoon salt
     1 pound bacon slices
     1 fresh lemon
     seafood sauce of choice

Lay the cleaned shrimp out on a platter and season them with spices and the juice from one lemon. Cut the bacon slices in half crosswise and wrap each shrimp with a strip of bacon using toothpicks to hold the rolled bacon in place. Arrange the rolled shrimp on a broiler pan with a rack so that the fat can drain to the lower pan. Cook under a broiler for approximately 20 minutes until the bacon is brown and crisp. Place the shrimp on a paper towel and allow them to cool. Once the excess fat has been removed transfer the shrimp onto a serving dish, arranging them attractively on the dish with a bowl of seafood sauce in the center.
Yield: 10 servings.

IRANIAN BULGUR-STUFFED FISH ROLLS

Fish rolls are fun to make and scrumptious to eat. Stuffing should be placed at the wide end of the filet. Starting at that end, roll as you would a jelly roll, securing it with a wooden toothpick to keep it together. Any fish that is easily filleted can be used, fresh or frozen. Our choice is sole.

>   4 4-ounce sole fillets
>   1¼ cups beef broth
>   ½ cup bulgur
>   ⅔ cup carrot, finely grated
>   ¼ cup sliced green onions
>   ¼ teaspoon orange peel, finely grated
>   dash each, salt, pepper and ground ginger
>   2 tablespoons frozen orange juice concentrate
>   1 tablespoon butter

Rinse fish, pat dry on paper towels.

Stuffing: In saucepan combine water and bulgur. Bring to boil, reduce heat, cover and simmer for 12 minutes. Stir in carrot and onion and cook 5 minutes longer. Drain off the excess liquid. Stir in the orange peel, salt and pepper.

Spoon ¼ cup of stuffing onto each fillet at widest end. Roll fish around filling and secure with a toothpick. Arrange fish rolls on a baking dish sprayed with a nonstick spray coating, seam side down. Place any extra stuffing around the rolls. In a small saucepan heat the orange juice concentrate, butter and ginger until the butter melts. Brush the liquid mixture over the fish rolls. Bake, uncovered, in a preheated 350° oven 20–25 minutes or until fish flakes easily when tested with a fork. Remove all toothpicks if placing on individual plates.
Yield: 4 servings.

VI

RICE & PASTA

*CITRUS WILD RICE

1 cup wild rice
2 large Florida oranges
⅓ cup Florida orange juice
⅓ cup raisins
2 tablespoons capers
1½ tablespoons olive oil
1½ tablespoons balsamic vinegar (or to taste)
salt and freshly ground black pepper
3 scallions, finely chopped
½ bunch flat leaf parsley, finely chopped (about ½ cup), plus
    4 sprigs for garnish

Rinse the rice thoroughly in cold water in a strainer. Place it in a large saucepan with 3 quarts water. Bring the rice to a boil, then reduce the heat and simmer the rice for 30 minutes. Remove the pan from the heat and let the rice stand until tender, about 30 minutes. Drain well in a colander and blot dry. Meanwhile, cut the oranges into segments. Cut off the rind (both zest and white pith) to expose the flesh. Make V-shaped cuts to remove the individual segments from the membranes. Dice most of the segments, reserving a few whole for garnish. Soak the raisins in the orange juice in mixing bowl for 5 minutes. Whisk the capers, olive oil, vinegar, salt, and pepper into the orange juice-raisin mixture. Stir in the scallions, chopped parsley, rice, and diced orange segments. Correct the seasoning, adding salt or vinegar to taste, Mound the rice on a platter or plates and decorate with the reserved whole orange segments and parsley sprigs.
Yield: 3–4 servings.

SHANGHAI RICE

This side dish provides an attractive burst of color to any meal. A favorite with youngsters of all ages.

11 ounces mandarin oranges, drained and coarsely chopped
½ cup chopped green onion
½ cup each, chopped red and green pepper
2 tablespoons olive oil
1 cup uncooked rice
1½ cups chicken broth
½ cup orange juice
¼ teaspoon salt
dash pepper

In large saucepan over medium heat, slowly sauté onion and peppers in oil just until tender. Be careful not to brown. Add rice, broth, orange juice, salt and pepper; bring to a boil. Reduce heat and simmer covered for 20 minutes or until liquid is absorbed and rice is done. Stir in oranges, cover and wait 5 minutes before serving.
Yield: 8 servings.

SUNSHINE & NUTTY RICE

Nutrients supplied by Mother Nature with few of empty calories. A healthy substitute for potatoes—flavorful too.

6 tablespoons butter
2 cups fresh squeezed orange juice, with pulp
1 cup water
2 teaspoons salt
1½ cups uncooked rice
½ cup almonds
⅓ cup chopped parsley

Combine butter, orange juice, water, salt and rice in large saucepan. Stir occasionally while bringing to boil. Reduce to medium heat, cover and cook undisturbed for 20 minutes or until liquid is absorbed and rice is tender. Remove from heat, leaving cover on. Toast almonds in small skillet over medium heat, stirring constantly until dark golden. Stir in almonds and parsley before serving.
Yield: 8 servings.

CONFETTI BAKE

We love recipes that lend themselves to variations providing us with choices to suit every mood and taste. The following easy-to-prepare dish does just that. Substitute boneless fish or meats, citrus and vegetables of choice and become a chef overnight. Makes a colorful presentation and leftovers are surprisingly good cold.

2 large, skinless, boneless chicken breasts, quartered
1 cup uncooked white rice
1 lime and 1 orange, sliced and seeded
¼ cup lemon juice, with pulp
¼ cup orange juice, with pulp
1 tablespoon each, lemon and orange rind, finely grated
1 can condensed, cream of celery soup
8 ounces frozen chopped spinach, cooked
½ cup beef bouillon
8 ounces milk
1 fresh carrot, grated
1 diced green onion
¼ cup fine bread crumbs
1 tablespoon each ground black pepper and paprika

Marinate chicken pieces in combination of lemon and orange juice for 20 minutes. Drain and set chicken aside. Mix together rice, juices, rinds, soup, bouillon, milk, onion and carrot in large bowl. Pour mixture into baking pan prepared with nonstick spray. Place chicken pieces throughout mixture, topping each piece with a lime or orange slice. Sprinkle with pepper, cover with aluminum foil and bake at 350º for 35 minutes. Remove foil, sprinkle with paprika and bread crumbs. Return to oven for an additional 30 minutes or until liquid begins to dry up and rice is cooked. Serve with green salad and basket of assorted bread sticks and biscuits.
Yield: 4 servings.

CHILLED MINI PENNE WITH ORANGE

One year after Easter, we came up with this unique way to use an over abundance of hard-boiled eggs. Since then, it has become traditional picnic fare all year long.

1 pound mini penne pasta, al dente
4 hard-boiled eggs, sliced
15-ounces whole baby corn
½ cup celery, chopped
1 cup red onion, chopped
½ cup oil-cured black olives
1 cup orange sections, with seeds and membranes removed
1 cup orange juice, with pulp
¼ teaspoon soy sauce
¼ teaspoon seasoned rice vinegar
¼ teaspoon white distilled vinegar
⅓ cup olive oil
¼ cup homemade mayo (optional)
1 teaspoon each salt, black pepper, oregano, and basil
½ teaspoon each crushed red pepper and lemon grass

Whisk together all liquids and set aside. Cool cooked pasta and place in large mixing bowl with tight lid. Combine all remaining ingredients and gently mix. Pour combined liquids over mixture and refrigerate overnight. Mix gently before serving.
Yield: 8 servings.

RIZ BORDOOCAN
(Orange-Rice)

This simple dish goes well with kabobs of all types.

1 cup white rice
1 cup water
1 tablespoon butter
2 cups fresh orange juice with pulp
1 cup orange sections
¼ teaspoon allspice, ground
½ teaspoon mint, chopped

Cook rice in medium size kettle. Add remaining ingredients, mix gently, cover, and simmer for ten minutes. Fluff before serving.
Yield: 4 servings.

BAKED SNAPPER STUFFED WITH ORANGE & ORZO

Because South Florida is blessed with a variety of fresh seafood and citrus all year long, we are encouraged to experiment with new combinations resulting in an array of recipes marrying the two food groups. It is a match made in heaven. Sometimes we will mix and match for a change. Try it!

    1 3- to 4-pound dressed snapper
    1 teaspoon salt
    1 teaspoon granulated garlic
    1 tablespoon olive oil

Wash the dressed fish and pat dry. Rub outside with oil, inside with salt and garlic.

Stuffing:
    1 cup orzo, precooked
    1 cup chopped celery
    ¼ cup chopped onion
    1 tablespoon dried parsley
    1 teaspoon ground allspice
    ½ cup orange juice, with pulp
    ¼ cup orange sections
    ½ cup water
    2 tablespoons lemon juice
    3 tablespoons olive oil
    1 lemon, sliced
    1 orange, sliced

Boil orzo, al dente. Drain to remove starch. Sauté celery and onion in 2 tablespoons oil to soften. Mix orzo, celery, parsley, allspice, onion, orange juice and sections, and water. Let rest 5 minutes. Gently flip ingredients. Stuff fish cavity, securing opening with wooden picks. Place fish in sprayed baking dish. Pour 1 tablespoon oil and 2 tablespoons lemon into dish for basting during baking. Bake in 350° oven for 45 minutes, or until fish flakes at fork test. Baste at least twice during baking. Transfer to warmed serving platter, remove picks and garnish with alternating lemon and orange slices.
Yield: 4 servings.

ITALIAN OIL & GARLIC
ANGEL HAIR WITH CITRUS

Oil and garlic over pasta has long been a staple in our family. Whether a side dish or entrée, adding citrus makes this traditional Italian dish new again.

    1 pound angel hair, al dente
    1½ cups olive oil
    12 large garlic cloves, sliced
    2 tablespoons dried basil
    1 tablespoon dried parsley
    1 cup black olives, sliced
    1 cup each orange and grapefruit sections
    2 cups locatelli cheese, coarsely grated

Sauté basil and sliced garlic in olive oil. Remove from heat and add olives. Pour over drained angel hair and toss in citrus sections and cheese. Sprinkle with parsley and serve.
Yield: 4 servings.

GREEK SPAGHETTI WITH CITRUS

The Greek version of the Italian oil & garlic standard is made with burned butter. We prefer it light in color and with citrus chunks of preference. (Frank favors the sweet orange and Marlene is partial to grapefruit. Either way adds succulence and extra to ordinary.)

    1 pound vermicelli, al dente
    1½ cups unsalted butter, melted (or darkened)
    3 tablespoons dried parsley
    2 cups citrus sections
    2 cups Romano cheese, coarsely grated

Toss cooked vermicelli into melted butter, carefully coating each strand. Sprinkle and toss in cheese, reserving ¼ cup. Pour onto serving platter, sprinkle with parsley and citrus sections. Sprinkle remaining cheese over all and serve.
Yield: 4 servings.

LEMON-GARLIC LINGUINI WITH SHRIMP

Combining pasta with shrimp provides a low-fat choice that is both delicious and surprisingly light. Enjoy it for a change of pace.

2 tablespoons butter
5 tablespoons olive oil
1 15-ounce can stewed tomatoes
6 cloves fresh garlic, minced
4 ounces lemon juice
¼ teaspoon salt
2 twists ground black pepper
8 ounces linguini, cooked al dente
¼ cup fresh parsley, chopped
2 tablespoons fresh lemon grass, snipped
2 pounds medium shrimp, peeled
fresh grated Romano cheese

In large skillet melt butter. Add 2 tablespoons oil and stewed tomatoes; heat for 2 minutes, stirring constantly. Add salt and pepper and simmer 2 minutes. Pour over cooked and drained linguini in deep pasta bowl; add parsley and lemon grass; toss and set aside. In large skillet heat 3 tablespoons olive oil and lemon juice. Add shrimp and garlic; sauté for 1 minute. Shake skillet regularly. Pour over linguini and sprinkle cheese over top. Serve immediately with basket of sliced Italian bread.
Yield: 4 servings.

LEMON SPINACH & TOMATO PASTA SALAD

The advent of the pasta salad has further increased the diversity of pasta uses. In the following, Aunt Jennie prefers spinach & tomato pasta but any can be used. Again, variations are endless, limited only by the imagination. Make your kitchen a food laboratory, letting your personal preferences serve as your guide.

12 ounces spinach, tomato and plain pasta, mixed
1 cup jumbo black olives, sliced
3½ ounces pepperoni, sliced
6 ripe plum tomatoes, diced
3 hard-boiled eggs, sliced (optional)
6 ounces Monterey Jack cheese chunks

⅓ cup fresh lemon juice
½ cup vegetable oil
¼ cup fresh basil, chopped
1 tablespoon oregano, dried
1 teaspoon crushed red pepper
salt and freshly ground black pepper to taste
sprigs of lemon mint or 1 lemon, sliced

Boil pasta al dente, drain and set aside to cool. Mix olives, pepperoni, tomatoes, and cheese in bowl. Blend together juice, zest, oil and spices for dressing. Toss olive mixture with cooled pasta. Pour dressing over and gently toss again. Garnish platter with sprigs of lemon mint or lemon slices.
Yield: 8 servings.

COUSCOUS WITH CITRUS

The precooked version of couscous (Middle Eastern semolina), is gaining in popularity with the busy homemaker looking for that healthy, easy, something different to serve. The following makes a side dish to accompany any entrée. As usual, Frank prefers the sweet orange and Marlene, the grapefruit. For fun, provide both. Viva la difference.

¾ cup plain couscous
2 chicken bouillon cubes
1¼ cups water
2 green onions, chopped
15 ounces black beans, cooked and drained
15 ounces green beans, French style, cooked and drained
1 tablespoon granulated garlic
¼ cup parsley, dried
2 cups fresh orange sections with juice
2 cups fresh grapefruit sections with juice

In medium saucepan, dissolve bouillon cubes in water. Once dissolved, bring to boil and stir in couscous, beans and seasonings. Cover, remove from heat and let stand 5 minutes. Fluff and serve immediately. Permit your guests to help themselves to toppings of oranges and grapefruit.
Yield: 6 servings

BREADS, DESSERTS & SWEETS

ENGLISH SUNSHINE TEA BREAD

You will want to make several of each. A favorite gift for school teachers and neighbors, twist loaf in colored plastic wrap.

2½ cups flour (all-purpose)
1½ teaspoons baking powder
½ teaspoon baking soda
½ teaspoon salt
½ cup butter or margarine (1 stick) softened
1¼ cups sugar
2 large eggs
6 ounces sour cream
¼ cup fresh lemon or orange juice
2 teaspoons freshly grated lemon or orange peel
¼ cup finely chopped nutmeats (optional)

Preheat the oven to 350º. Grease a loaf pan and dust lightly with flour. Stir together the flour, baking powder, baking soda and salt. In another bowl beat the butter until smooth. Add peel and sugar, beating to creamy texture. Beat while adding the eggs, slowly and one at a time, until thoroughly blended. Scrape the sides and bottom of bowl regularly to insure complete blending. Alternate adding sour cream and flour mixture until both are well blended. Slowly stir in juice, and nutmeats if desired. Spoon the batter into the loaf pan, baking 65 minutes or until toothpick or cake tester inserted in center comes out clean. Allow loaf to set (in pan) five minutes on wire rack before removing from pan and cooling completely on wire rack.
Yield: 1 loaf.

TANGERINE/SWEET POTATO CUPCAKES

Moving sweet potatoes from the vegetable course to dessert can be the coup of the season. This untraditional alternative provides a moist, sweet prelude to the flavor of holidays. Satsuma oranges may be substituted for tangerine. A bed and breakfast presentation is to use mini-cup cake tins and serve a basket with afternoon coffee or tea.

    1 pound sweet potatoes, scrubbed and pierced
    2 cups all-purpose flour
    2 teaspoons baking powder
    1¼ teaspoons baking soda
    1 teaspoon powdered ginger
    ¾ teaspoon salt
    ⅓ cup fat-free milk
    1 tablespoon tangerine peel, finely grated
    ⅓ cup tangerine juice
    3 tablespoons orange liqueur
    1 teaspoon vanilla extract
    ¼ cup butter, softened
    ¼ cup vegetable oil
    1 cup, firmly packed, dark brown sugar
    2 eggs

Coat cupcake pans with a nonstick spray. Dust them lightly with flour and set them aside. Preheat the oven to 375°. Place the potatoes in a medium saucepan and simmer uncovered for approximately 20 minutes or until the flesh can be penetrated easily with a fork, then purée them and set them aside. In separate small bowls, mix together the dry ingredients and then the moist ingredients then set both aside. In a large bowl, beat the butter and oil until creamy. Gradually add sugar, beating until fluffy. Slowly mix in the eggs one at a time until blended. Add a third of the flour mixture and stir well. Continue to add flour and milk mixtures until blended. Stir in sweet potato purée and fill each cupcake recess two thirds full. Bake for 20 minutes or until inserted cake tester comes out clean. Allow to cool for 5 minutes before removing from the pan. Cool on a wire rack. Arrange cupcakes on a dollied serving platter; drizzle with glaze. Garnish with orange-tinged coconut if desired. **Yield: 1½ dozen cupcakes.**

ORANGE PECANS

Important Safety Hint: Candy making requires high heat and if the liquid splashes onto skin during boiling, it will adhere, causing severe burns. Keep children away from area while making candy.

> 1½ cups sugar
> ½ cup water
> 1 orange, juice squeezed (with pulp), rind finely grated
> 3 cups shelled pecan halves

Dissolve the sugar, orange juice and water in a heavy saucepan (avoid aluminum). Place on high heat and stir constantly until the mixture comes to a boil. When the syrup begins to crystallize around the edges of the pan, remove from the heat and add rind and nuts. Keep turning the nuts in the syrup until all sides are fully coated. Pour onto wax paper and leave to cool. When cool, crack into hunks. Store in paper cups or waxed paper.
Yield: 1½ pounds candy.

GRAPEFRUIT-PINEAPPLE PIE

Here's a gift from the tropics that everyone will love.

> 1 9-inch pastry shell, baked and cooled
> 1 cup flaked coconut, toasted and divided
> 8 ounces canned crushed pineapple
> 2 envelopes natural gelatin
> 1½ cups grapefruit sections, divided
> 14 ounce can sweetened condensed milk
> 2 egg whites
> ¼ teaspoon cream of tartar
> 6 sprigs fresh spearmint

Toast the coconut by spreading it out in a shallow pan, and baking at 350° in a preheated oven for 8 to 12 minutes (stir often) until golden. Measuring the juice, drain the pineapple. Add enough water to measure ¼ cup. Dissolve the gelatin in the pineapple juice using low heat stirring constantly. Slice 2 cups grapefruit sections into small pieces. Mix together the grapefruit pieces, crushed pineapple and condensed milk. Stir in the gelatin mixture and set it aside. Beat

the egg whites and cream of tartar in a small bowl until peaks begin to form. Fold into the grapefruit mixture. Sprinkle ½ cup of the toasted coconut in the bottom of a prepared pastry shell. Spoon the grapefruit mixture over the coconut and chill until firm. Before serving, garnish with remaining grapefruit sections and remaining ½ cup toasted coconut. Serve slices on chilled plates with a sprig of spearmint atop for an elegant presentation.
Yield: 8 slices.

MOUSSE D'ORANGE

Delicious and creamy, the light whipped texture is the perfect dessert after a large meal. Serve it with a cup of hot rich coffee.

1 envelope natural gelatin
4 large mandarins or tangelos, rind grated, juice squeezed
6 eggs, separated
¾ cup sugar
1 cup heavy cream
¼ teaspoon salt

Prepare a 9-inch soufflé dish by cutting a 3-inch-wide band of wax paper long enough to fit around the top. Tie it around the dish so it protrudes about 2 inches over the rim. Stir the gelatin into 3 tablespoons of mandarin juice and set it aside to soften. Beat the egg yolks with ½ cup of the sugar until the mixture is foaming and pale. Beat in the rest of the juice then transfer the mixture to the top of a double boiler and simmer over moderate heat, stirring constantly with a wooden spoon until the mixture coats the spoon. Do not allow it to boil. Remove the pan from the heat and stir in the softened gelatin. Pour the mixture into a bowl and stir in the grated rind then allow it to cool. Whip the cream until it is thick but not stiff. Beat the egg whites with the salt into stiff peaks. Fold the cream into the egg yolk mixture. Gently fold in the egg whites. Pour the mixture into the prepared soufflé dish. It should come over the rim and to the level of the wax paper. Refrigerate for at least 8 hours or overnight. Transfer soufflé by inverting soufflé dish over deep serving bowl. Remove wax paper and garnish rim of bowl with mandarins, thinly sliced and halved.
Yield: 6 to 8 servings.

ORANGE CUSTARD

The natural sweetness of orange combined with the creaminess of custard makes this a consummate delight to the discerning palate.

⅓ cup sugar
3 tablespoons cornstarch
1 cup light cream or half-and-half
4 egg yolks, beaten
⅓ cup orange juice
1 tablespoon grated orange peel
1 cup fresh orange pieces, peeled and seeded
9 small leaves of fresh spearmint

Mix the sugar and the cornstarch together in the top of a double boiler. Over low heat, gradually add light cream while stirring constantly until the mixture thickens, then remove it from the heat. Stir in the beaten egg yolks, orange juice and peel. Return to heat stirring constantly until thickened, about 4 minutes. Pour into custard cups or champagne glasses and chill until it sets. Before serving, place cup or glass in center of saucer, circle with orange pieces. Dot center of custard with a leaf or two of fresh spearmint to set it off.
Yield: 6 cups.

VALERIE'S FROSTY KEY LARGO KEY LIME PIE

Here's a dessert that fits the ambiance of the Florida Keys. So easy to put together, it can be a last-minute decision that tastes like it took hours to prepare.

8 ounces light cool whip
1 can condensed milk
½ cup key lime juice
ready made graham cracker pie crust
4 slivers fresh lime

Combine together in a medium mixing bowl the cool whip, condensed milk, and key lime juice and mix together. Pour the mixture into the pie crust, garnish the top with lime slices, and place in the freezer. Remove from the freezer 5 minutes before serving.
Yield: 6 servings.

DANISH CITRUS/YOGURT COMPOTE

Whether for breakfast or dessert, the following compote suggests the best of all seasons. Granola adds substance to the smooth and creamy tang of citrus and yogurt. Pucker up and enjoy something different.

sections and juice of 2 large, pink grapefruit
sections and juice of 2 navel oranges
1 tablespoon finely grated lemon peel
¼ cup lemon juice
3 tablespoons light brown sugar
½ teaspoon finely ground cinnamon
¼ teaspoon finely ground nutmeg
¼ teaspoon finely ground allspice
8 ounces fresh or frozen whole cranberries
1 quart low-fat plain yogurt
1 cup granola
6 small sprigs of lemon mint

Set citrus sections aside in the refrigerator until they are chilled. Bring the mixture of citrus juices, cranberries, sugar, spices and peel to a boil. Reduce the heat and simmer for 10 minutes or until the sugar is melted and the cranberries pop. Allow to cool to room temperature, then add the chilled citrus sections. Divide the yogurt into six individual serving bowls. Top each with an equal share of fruit mixture then allow to chill in the refrigerator. Just before serving sprinkle equal amounts of granola atop each compote. Garnish with sprig of lemon mint.
Yield: 6 servings.

LEMON MERINGUE PIE

Decades of preparation have taught us three "secrets" when preparing this favorite: spreading meringue over warm filling will eliminate "weeping" after baking, adding lemon juice after filling is cooked adds to the distinctive flavor and spreading the meringue to the edge of the crust will prevent shrinkage. Our grandmothers did the work, now this fool-proof method is ours to enjoy.

> 1½ cups sugar
> 3 tablespoons cornstarch
> 3 tablespoons all-purpose flour
> pinch salt
> 1½ cups hot water
> 3 eggs, yolks and whites separated
> ½ teaspoon grated lemon peel
> 2 tablespoons margarine or butter
> ⅓ cup lemon juice
> 1 9-inch pastry shell, baked
> 1 teaspoon lemon juice
> 6 tablespoons sugar

In a large saucepan combine 1 cup of sugar, cornstarch, flour and salt and mix well. Gradually stir in the water and on high heat bring the mixture to a boil, stirring constantly. Reduce the heat and continue stirring then allow to simmer for 8 minutes. Remove the mixture from the heat. Beat egg yolks and fold in a small amount of hot mixture, then return to the hot mixture and bring to a boil over medium heat, stirring constantly. Reduce the heat and allow to simmer an additional 4 minutes. Remove from the heat and add the peel, butter and gradually stir in the lemon juice. Cover the pan with plastic wrap and set it aside while preparing the meringue.

Meringue: Beat egg whites with 1 teaspoon of lemon juice until soft peaks form. Beat in remaining ½ cup of sugar, two tablespoons at a time; beat until stiff peaks form and all sugar is dissolved.

Pour the warm filling into a cooled baked pastry shell and spread the meringue over the warm filling, sealing at pastry edges. Bake at 350° for approximately 12–15 minutes or until the meringue is golden. Allow to cool on a wire rack at room temperature for 1 hour. Chill thoroughly to set, 3–6 hours, before serving. Dip the knife into warm or cool water and shake off the excess before slicing.

Yield: 8 servings.

ORANGE CHARLOTTE

Although this old-fashioned favorite can be served alone, try pouring it over vanilla or dark chocolate wafers.

    ½ cup sugar
    1 cup carbonated orange soda
    1 medium egg white, beaten stiff
    2 tablespoons gelatin
    2 tablespoons fresh lemon juice

Place the gelatin in ⅓ cup of cool water and dissolve it over boiling water, stirring constantly until it is fully dissolved. Add the lemon juice and the sugar to the gelatin mixture, and allow the mixture to cool. Once the liquid has cooled add the orange soda, and fold in the egg white. Beat the mixture well until it stiffens. Pour the well blended mixture into individual serving cups and allow them to chill in the refrigerator before serving.
Yield: 4-5 servings.

FANCY FRUITS GRANDE

Looking for something delectable but not too sweet? The contrasting richness of Grand Marnier and the natural tartness of fruit make perfect companions. Oranges like mercots or honeybells work best for this dish because they are naturally sweet, easy to peel, and available in seedless varieties. Explore new worlds by substituting strawberries, blueberries, or raspberries for mixed berries.

    2 cups fresh or frozen mixed berries, thawed
    whipped cream topping
    4 teaspoons Grand Marnier liqueur
    10 or 12 whole fresh mint leaves
    2 seedless oranges

Peel the oranges and separate them into individual sections insuring that there are no seeds. Arrange the sections in a pinwheel shape or circle on each individual serving plate. Top the orange slices with ½ cup of mixed berries then drizzle each with 1 teaspoon of Grand Marnier. Top the fruit mixture with whipped cream and garnish with 3 or 4 mint leaves. Serve cold.
Yield: 4 servings.

EVERYTHING NICE COOKIES

No meal is complete without something sweet to top it off. The following cookies fit the bill, whether you choose the basic spice cookie plain or dressed up with lemon frosting. Bet you can't limit yourself to just one.

1 cup sugar
1 egg
¾ cup shortening
¼ cup orange blossom honey
2 cups all-purpose flour
1 teaspoon baking soda
1½ teaspoons ginger
1 teaspoon ground cinnamon
¾ teaspoon ground cloves
½ teaspoon salt

Lemon Frosting:
2 cups confectioner's sugar
3 tablespoons butter, softened
1 teaspoon grated lemon peel
4 tablespoons lemon juice

Cream together in a large mixing bowl the shortening and sugar. Add to the shortening mixture the egg and blend well, then beat in the honey. Combine all of the dry ingredients and add to the creamed mixture, then mix well. Drop by rounded teaspoonfuls onto greased baking sheets. Bake at 350º for 8-10 minutes. Remove to wire racks and allow to cool.

Frosting: Cream the sugar, butter and lemon peel. Gradually add lemon juice, beating until frosting reaches spreading consistency. Frost cookies.

Yield: about 4 dozen cookies.

TURKISH GLAZED ALMOND STUFFED DATES

A Middle Eastern favorite, these sugar glazed stuffed dates are very rich. Serve them on a large attractive platter garnished with fresh lemon slices and hot Arabic coffee.

    2 pounds pitted dates
    5 whole cloves
    1 cup white sugar
    2 cups water
    ½ teaspoon fresh lemon juice
    ½ cup whole blanched almonds

In a medium saucepan add the water, sugar, and cloves and bring the mixture to a boil. Stir the mixture constantly until the sugar is fully dissolved then reduce the heat to low and simmer uncovered until the liquid reduces to a thick syrupy consistency. Remove the pitted dates from the container and stuff each with an almond, dip it into the syrup then allow it to dry. Once all of the dates have been stuffed and glazed, sprinkle them with fresh lemon juice and serve.

SOUR ORANGE PIE

Juice from the sour orange, which alone is extremely tangy, is tamed by the cream cheese and condensed milk. The end result is a pie filling with the taste of old-fashioned orange juice and vanilla ice cream bars. Presqueezed sour orange juice may be difficult to find, but fresh sour oranges can usually be obtained at most produce stores.

    1¼ ounces sweetened condensed milk
    ½ cup sour orange juice
    2 large egg yolks
    8 ounces cream cheese
    1 premade graham cracker pie crust

In a blender combine and mix well the condensed milk, orange juice, egg yolks, and cream cheese until the mixture is thoroughly blended and the consistency becomes thick. Pour the mixture into the ready-made pie crust then place the pie in the refrigerator to chill for at least one hour.

Yield: 1 pie

ORANGE BLOSSOM MUFFINS

Suitable for Sunday Brunch or a warm greeting to new neighbors.

    2 cups biscuit mix
    ¼ cup sugar
    1 large egg, lightly beaten
    2 tablespoons vegetable oil
    ½ cup orange marmalade
    ½ cup chopped pecans
    3 tablespoons sugar
    1 tablespoon all-purpose flour
    ½ teaspoon ground cinnamon
    ¼ teaspoon ground nutmeg

Combine in a large mixing bowl the biscuit mix and ¼ cup sugar making a well in the center of the mixture. Add the egg, orange juice and oil to the dry mixture stirring until moistened. Stir in the marmalade and pecans. Once thoroughly mixed spoon the batter into muffin tins lined with baking cups, filling them about two-thirds full. Sprinkle the muffins with a mixture of 3 tablespoons sugar, 1 tablespoon flour, ½ teaspoon cinnamon and ¼ teaspoon nutmeg, then bake at 400° for approximately twenty minutes or until golden.
Yield: 1 dozen.

SCOTCH/IRISH SWEET 'N NUTTY

Imagine a New England winter day at Grandma's house. The rich, warm aroma of this simple out-of-the-past dessert can only be surpassed by its memory-evoking flavor.

    4 cups toasted bread cubes
    3 large eggs
    1½ cups light cream
    1 tablespoon orange peel
    ½ cup orange juice, with pulp
    ¼ cup light brown sugar
    ¼ cup granulated sugar
    1 teaspoon vanilla
    ½ cup maple syrup
    ⅓ cup toasted pecan pieces

Spice Bag: Place 2 cinnamon sticks, ½ teaspoon whole cloves, and ½ teaspoon whole allspice in square piece of cheesecloth. Tie the corners to seal.

Beat the eggs then stir in the cream, sugars (crush all lumps), vanilla and orange peel, mix until just combined. Divide the bread cubes equally among 4 individual (10 ounce) casserole crocks. Distribute the egg mixture equally over the bread cubes, then bake at 350° for 30 minutes or until a knife inserted in the center comes out clean. While the crocks are cooling, combine the orange juice, maple syrup, ⅓ cup water and spice bag in saucepan. Heat to boiling, reduce the heat, cover and simmer for 10 minutes. Squeeze the spice bag against the side of the pan to drain and remove. Simmer, uncovered, for an additional 10 minutes to permit reduction of the liquid. Stir in the pecans and spoon the sauce over the warm pudding. Best if served immediately. A dollop of whipped cream sprinkled with ground cinnamon may be added.
Yield: 4 servings.

VALHALLA AMBROSIA

Refreshing and beautiful, this food of the Gods provides a healthy finish to any meal.

  2 tablespoons sugar
  2 tablespoons water
  2 tablespoons orange juice
  1½ teaspoons lemon juice
  2 tablespoons kirsch
  ½ diced medium pineapple
  1 medium grapefruit
  1½ large oranges, diced
  2 medium apples, diced
  ½ pound bananas, sliced
  ½ cup shredded coconut

Combine together in a saucepan the sugar, water, orange juice, lemon juice and kirsch and stir until the sugar dissolves. Add the fruits until all are covered with syrup. Heap in dessert glasses and sprinkle with coconut. Serve well chilled.
Yield: 6 servings.

NORTH-SOUTH CAKE

The combined flavors of New England cranberries with citrus unite to create a unique and memorable taste. Since family members like this glazed and unglazed, nutty and nutless, I sometimes drizzle glaze over one half the cake and sprinkle crushed pecans over one half of each side. Beats baking four cakes and pleases everybody. Great with coffee or fresh milk.

Hint: Have all ingredients at room temperature.

½ cup fresh or frozen cranberries
¼ cup fresh orange juice
2 tablespoons finely grated orange peel
2 tablespoons orange blossom honey
2⅔ cups all-purpose flour
1 teaspoon baking powder
1 teaspoon baking soda
pinch salt
1½ sticks unsalted butter
1 tablespoon packed brown sugar
4 large eggs
1 teaspoon lemon or orange extract
1¼ cups sour cream

Optional Glaze:
2 tablespoons orange marmalade
½ cup confectioner's sugar, sifted
1 tablespoon fresh orange juice
½ cup crushed pecans (optional)

Simmer the cranberries and orange juice over medium heat until the cranberries pop and the juice is nearly gone. Stir frequently and allow to cool, then dice. Grease and lightly flour a bundt pan, position rack in the lower third of the oven and preheat at 325º. Combine the peel, sugar and honey with the cranberries. Mix together in a separate bowl, the flour, baking soda, baking powder and salt. Beat butter, eggs and brown sugar until smooth, then add the orange extract. Gradually fold in the dry ingredients, alternating with sour cream. Mix until blended. Spread one third of the batter around the bundt pan. Pour half the cranberry mixture atop; repeat.

Top with the remaining batter. Bake approximately one hour or until inserted cake tester is retrieved clean. Allow to cool in the pan on a wire rack set over waxed paper for 10 minutes. Turn the cake out onto a rack, finish cooling before transferring to a serving plate.
Glaze: In small saucepan, warm marmalade and orange juice; stir in confectioner's sugar until smooth. Drizzle over cake as desired.
Yield: 16 servings.

CITRUS CHIFFON PIE

Sweet and tangy, the perfect dessert after any meal.

    1 tablespoon natural gelatin
    ½ cup sugar
    pinch salt
    4 eggs, yolks and whites separated
    ½ cup lemon juice
    ½ cup orange juice
    ¼ cup water
    ½ teaspoon orange peel
    ½ teaspoon lemon peel
    ⅓ cup sugar
    1 9-inch pastry shell, baked

In a saucepan mix together the gelatin, ½ cup sugar and salt. Beat together the egg yolks, juices and water, then add it to the saucepan. Cook and stir gently until the mixture begins to boil. Remove from the heat and stir in the peel. Allow the mixture to cool, stirring occasionally until the mixture begins to thicken. Beat the egg whites until soft peaks form. Add ⅓ cup of sugar and beat to stiff peaks. Fold meringue into the chilled gelatin mixture. Heap the combination into a cooled shell and chill until firm. Garnish with whipped topping and thin slices of citrus twists. Slice with chilled knife.
Yield: 8 servings.

NORTH CAROLINA POUND CAKE

While attending college at the University of Miami, in Coral Gables, Florida, Valerie was fortunate to room with three generous girls from North Carolina who shared their boxes of baked goods sent from home. Her favorite to this day is the following pound cake prepared by her roommates' mother.

> 1½ cups all-purpose flour
> 3 teaspoons baking powder
> ½ teaspoon salt
> 1½ cup sugar
> ¾ cup orange juice
> ¾ cup vegetable oil
> 2 teaspoons lemon extract
> 4 eggs
> ¼ cup sour cream

Preheat the oven to 325°. Lightly grease and dust a bundt pan with finely sifted powdered sugar. Sift first 3 ingredients together 3 times into large bowl. Add all remaining ingredients and mix well. Bake at 325° for 45 minutes or until inserted cake tester comes out clean.

Glaze:
1½ cups of powdered sugar
½ cup lemon juice

Spoon half of glaze over hot cake. Let sit 10 minutes. Invert onto serving plate and spoon remaining glaze over cake. Cool before slicing. **Yield: 16 slices.**

ITALIAN GRILLED GRAPEFRUIT WITH RASPBERRIES & AMARETTO

Grilling grapefruit sounded strange until we tried it. It's not only great tasting, but appearancewise, quite impressive.

> 3 large pink grapefruit
> 3 tablespoons dark brown sugar
> ½ cup fresh raspberries
> Amaretto liqueur

Preheat the broiler oven then slice the grapefruit in half crosswise and remove all of the seeds. Seedless varieties of grapefruit are available that make the task easier. With a citrus knife cut around the inside of each individual grapefruit section so that it can be easily removed from the skin. Pour ½ tablespoon of liqueur and ½ tablespoon of brown sugar over each of the grapefruit halves then place the grapefruit halves (cut side up) on a baking tray then place in the oven. Cook the grapefruit halves under the broiler just until the sugar melts and the edges of the fruit become slightly brown, approximately 10 minutes. When done remove immediately and garnish each of the halves with fresh raspberries. Serve hot.
Yield: 6 servings.

FRENCH ORANGE CITRUS SORBET

Looking for a 100% natural dessert? This is real sorbet—not a chemically concocted reproduction. Only fresh fruit juice and honey are used.

> 2 cups fresh orange juice
> ½ cup honey
> 1 whole orange, preferably seedless
> 1 tablespoon lemon juice

Grate 1 teaspoon of rind from the orange then place the rind in a large mixing bowl and add the orange juice, honey, and lemon juice. Blend the mixture well by stirring then pour into small serving bowls, and place them in the freezer until frozen solid. When ready to serve, top each with seedless fresh orange segments.
Yield: 4 servings

*FROZEN ORANGE SWIRL PIE

A snappy gingersnap crust complements the flavor of the ice-cream pie.

¼ cup sugar
4 teaspoons cornstarch
¾ cup frozen Florida orange juice concentrate, thawed
⅓ cup water
2 tablespoons margarine or butter, cut up
1 tablespoon finely shredded Florida orange peel
1¼ cups finely crushed gingersnaps
⅓ cup margarine or butter, melted
6 cups vanilla frozen yogurt or low-fat or light vanilla
  ice cream
fresh mint sprigs (optional)

For sauce, in a medium saucepan combine sugar and cornstarch; stir in thawed orange juice concentrate and water. Cook and stir over medium heat until thickened and bubbly. Cook and stir for 2 minutes more. Remove from heat; stir in the 2 tablespoons margarine or butter and orange peel. Cover and cool completely.

For crust, in a medium bowl combine crushed ginger snaps and the ⅓ cup melted margarine. Toss to mix well. Spread mixture evenly into a 9-inch pie plate. Press onto bottom and sides to form a firm, even crust. Chill about 1 hour or until firm.

Place 4 cups of the frozen yogurt or ice cream into a chilled bowl. Using a wooden spoon, stir the yogurt to soften slightly. Spoon the softened yogurt into the crumb crust. Drizzle half of the cool orange sauce over the yogurt. Swirl sauce into the yogurt with a knife or narrow metal spatula.

Remove remaining 2 cups of frozen yogurt from the freezer. Make small scoops of yogurt with a small ice-cream dipper and arrange over pie. (Or use a spoon to make small scoops of yogurt.) Do not smooth top evenly. Drizzle the remaining orange sauce over all. Cover and freeze at least 8 hours before serving. If desired, garnish with mint springs.

Makes 8 servings.

CITRUS SLICES WITH POMEGRANATE

Pomegranates are actually berries containing delicious sweetly-tart seeds that are outstanding sprinkled over all types of fruit dishes or salads. Be careful with the juice, however—the stain is permanent.

2 large fresh grapefruit, peeled and separated
4 ounces fresh orange juice
fresh pomegranate seeds
2 ounces pomegranate syrup
fresh mint leaves

Remove the seeds from the grapefruit sections then place them on a large serving plate. In a small mixing bowl combine and mix together the orange juice and pomegranate syrup then pour the liquid over the grapefruit slices. Sprinkle pomegranate seeds over the tops and garnish each with fresh mint leaves. Serve cold.
Yield: 4 servings.

ORANGE BAVARIAN CREAM

Refreshing and light, a triumph for the palate.

1 tablespoon gelatin
¼ cup cold water
¾ cup orange juice with pulp
½ tablespoons lemon juice
½ teaspoon orange rind, finely grated
⅓ cup sugar
¼ teaspoon salt
1 egg white
½ cup cream, whipped

Soak the gelatin in water for 2 minutes. Heat the fruit juices and rind with half of the sugar until it dissolves. Slowly add and dissolve the gelatin in the hot juice then allow to chill in the refrigerator until partly set. Add salt to the egg white and beat until the mixture is stiff. Continue beating while adding the remaining sugar in a steady stream. Beat until glossy. Fold the egg white mixture and cream into the gelatin mixture. Pour into a mold and chill until firm. Garnish with orange twists.

ORANGE FILLING

Treat your taste buds to a burst of tropical sunshine with the refreshing flavor of tangy orange.

5 large eggs
3 egg yolks
½ cup sugar
5 tablespoons frozen orange juice concentrate, thawed and
    diluted
2 tablespoons orange rind, finely grated
⅛ teaspoon salt
1 cup unsalted butter, cut into small pieces
2 tablespoons Grand Marnier
orange rind strips for garnish

In the top section of a double boiler, combine the eggs, yolks, sugar, orange juice and rind, then bring to a boil. Reduce the heat to low and stir constantly with a wire whisk until thickened. Continue stirring while adding the butter, a few pieces at a time. Remove from the heat and stir in the Grand Marnier. Transfer to a glass bowl for cooling. Serve in custard cups or use as filling in a cake. Garnish with orange strips.
Yield: 3 cups.

KEY LIME FILLING

This South Florida favorite is presented on spice cake.

2 cups sugar
1 cup butter, cut in pieces
⅔ cup fresh key lime juice
1 tablespoon key lime rind, finely grated
4 large eggs, slightly beaten
fresh mint sprigs for garnish

In the top of double boiler, combine the sugar, butter, a piece at a time, lime juice and rind. Cook over medium heat, stirring constantly until the butter has totally melted. Gradually stir in the eggs, one at a time. Cook over low heat, stirring constantly until the mixture thickens, then remove from the heat and allow to cool.

Transfer to a glass bowl, cover and chill at least 2 hours. Garnish with mint sprigs when serving.
Yield: 3 cups.

CITRUS FILLING

This luscious option blends several citrus flavors. One advantage to living in Florida is the accessibility to citrus trees. A gentle rub of lemon leaves just prior to serving will issue a trace of lemon scent bringing the outdoors to your table.

> 5 large egg yolks
> 1¼ cups orange juice
> 2 tablespoons lime juice
> 2 tablespoons lemon juice
> ¾ cup confectioner's sugar
> 1 envelope plain gelatin
> 1 tablespoon finely grated orange rind
> 1 tablespoon finely grated lemon rind
> 1 tablespoon finely grated lime rind
> 1 cup heavy cream
> 1 orange, sliced
> 5 lemon leaves

Dissolve the gelatin in a bowl with the combined juices. In the top of a double boiler, whisk in the egg yolks, confectioner's sugar, and salt. Add the juices and gelatin mixture. Cook slowly, stirring until the gelatin is completely dissolved and the mixture begins to thicken. Remove from the heat and fold in rinds. Refrigerate to cool and thicken further. Whip cream until stiff and fold into orange mixture until well blended. Spoon into sherbet glasses and refrigerate 2 hours, or until set. Garnish with orange slices and lemon leaves.
Yield: 8 servings.

*ORANGE ANGEL CAKE

Using orange juice concentrate in place of some of the water in the angel cake mix gives this cake a delicate orange flavor and color.

> 1 15-ounce or 16-ounce package angel cake mix
> ¾ cup frozen Florida orange juice concentrate, thawed
> 1 8-ounce container frozen light whipped dessert topping, thawed
> ½ cup plain low-fat yogurt
> citrus roses (optional)

Prepare angel cake as directed on the package, except pour ⅓ cup of the thawed orange juice concentrate into a 2-cup measure; add enough water to the concentrate for the mixture to equal the amount of water called for in the package directions. Continue with package directions, baking the batter in an ungreased 10" tube pan according to package directions. Immediately invert cake (leave in pan) and allow it to cool completely.

Loosen the sides of the cake from the pan and remove the cake from the pan. For topping, in a medium bowl gently stir together the thawed topping and yogurt. Fold in remaining orange juice concentrate. Spread topping mixture over top and sides of cake. If desired, garnish with citrus roses made from grapefruit or orange peel. Store in the refrigerator.
Makes 12 to 16 servings.

Citrus Rose: Cut the peel from stem end of a Florida orange or grapefruit, forming a circular base (do not sever). Continue cutting a strip of peel about ¾" to 1" wide in a spiral motion to opposite end of fruit, making one long, continuous strip and slicing thinly (do not cut into white membrane). Start coiling strip tightly, beginning at end opposite base. Coil the strip onto the base to form a rose. Garnish with mint leaves and small strips of peel, if desired.

FRENCH LEMON LAYER CAKE

A light and fluffy cake layered with flavor.

> 1 1-pound cake loaf, sliced into ⅜-inch thick pieces
> 1 cup butter
> 2 cups powdered sugar
> grated lemon peel and juice from 2 large lemons
> 2 eggs, separated
> ⅔ cup whipping cream
> 2 tablespoons Marsala wine
> whipped cream
> grated lemon peel

Combine together in a medium mixing bowl the butter, 1¾ cups powdered sugar, and the lemon peel and mix until light and fluffy. Whip the two egg yolks and add in one at a time, then continue whisking and add half the lemon juice. In a second mixing bowl beat the cream until soft peaks form then fold the whipped cream into the lemon butter mixture. In a mixing bowl beat the egg whites until stiff peaks form, then fold the beaten egg whites into the lemon mixture. In a small mixing bowl, combine the remaining lemon juice and the Marsala wine, then stir. On a 9- by 5-inch baking pan lay out a layer of cake slices, then sprinkle each with a little of the Marsala mixture, and spoon on a third of the lemon mixture. Repeat alternating layers of cake and mixtures ending with a layer of cake. (There should be 3 layers of lemon mixture and 4 layers of cake when done.) Place cake in the refrigerator until well chilled. To serve, invert the cake on a serving plate and remove the pan. Top with whipped cream and grated lemon peel.

Yield: 8 servings

CINNAMON ORANGE SLICES

This is a great accompaniment for spicy roasts and red meat dishes.
Because it is very sweet, serve it moderately.

juice from 1 lemon
½ cup water
1½ cups granulated sugar
3 fresh oranges
2 cinnamon sticks

In a medium sauce pan on medium heat blend together the sugar,
water, lemon juice and cinnamon and cook it until it achieves a
syrupy consistency. Set it aside. Wash the oranges well in cool water
then slice each into eight slices and remove all of the seeds. Place the
orange slices into the hot syrup (with the rind) and bring the
mixture to a boil on high heat. Reduce the heat to medium and allow
the mixture to cook uncovered until the rinds become clear. After the
mixture has cooled place it in the refrigerator to chill. Serve cold.
Yield: 3-4 servings

BANANA SPLIT ICE CREAM

An old-fashioned favorite made a new way.

3 mashed bananas
1 cup orange juice
⅓ cup lemon juice
3 cups sugar
2 large cans evaporated milk
1 quart whole milk
1 small can crushed pineapple
1 small jar chopped maraschino cherries
½ cup chopped roasted pecans (unsalted)

Set aside the nuts and whole milk. Mix together the remaining
ingredients in a freezer tub. Pour in enough whole milk to reach the
freezer mark. Follow the usual freezing procedure. When the process
is nearly finished, add the nuts and complete the freeze.
Yield: 8 servings

*CITRUS CHOCOLATE FUDGE CAKE

A rich chocolate citrus flavor and an attractive presentation.

2 ounces semisweet chocolate, chopped
3 ounces cream cheese
1 package (18.25 ounces) devil's food cake mix (with
    pudding in the mix)
1 teaspoon cinnamon
3 eggs
1 cup Florida grapefruit juice
½ cup corn oil
2 tablespoons orange liqueur
1 12-ounce package semisweet mini chocolate chips
¾ cup finely chopped pecans

Glaze:
3 ounces semisweet chocolate, chopped
1 tablespoon butter

Heat the oven to 350º. Grease and flour a 12-cup ring pan. Melt the
chocolate and cream cheese in a 2-quart saucepan over low heat. Stir
until blended then set aside to cool. Place the cake mix and cinnamon in mixing bowl. In a medium bowl, whisk together the eggs,
grapefruit juice, corn oil and orange liqueur. Add to cake mix along
with the cooled chocolate mixture. Beat about 3 minutes, then stir in
the chips and pecans. Pour into the pan and bake 55 to 60 minutes,
or until the cake tests done. Let sit in the pan 10 minutes before
removing to rack to cool.
FOR GLAZE: Melt 3 ounces of chocolate and butter in 1½-quart
saucepan. Stir until blended. Drizzle over cooled cake. Allow glaze
to set before serving.
Serves 10 to 12.

FRUIT & NUT STUFFED ORANGE RINDS

Various combinations of fruit and nuts are a staple of Middle East cuisine. Fancy, unusual, colorful and delicious, these stuffed orange skins will make you famous with your guests.

> 3 fresh oranges
> 1 tablespoon white sugar
> ½ cup water
> 2 tablespoons pecans, chopped
> 1 cup seedless green grapes
> 1 tablespoon walnuts, chopped

Wash the oranges well under cool running water then slice them in half crosswise and remove the orange sections inside of each. In a large mixing bowl combine the orange sections (with seeds removed), grapes, sugar, walnuts, and pecans and stir the mixture well. Once the mixture is well blended fill the empty orange rinds with it then place them on the rack of a pressure cooker. Add the water and cook the stuffed orange rinds just until cooking pressure is reached, then cool the cooker at once by holding it under cool running water. Allow the stuffed rinds to chill in the refrigerator before serving.
Yield: 6 servings

MANDARIN ORANGE CHEESE PIE

This is one of Frank's all-time favorite desserts. The mandarin orange is a naturally sweet and juicy one that contains less acid than other oranges. Here its tangy taste is used to enhance smooth creamy cheese, producing an unusual but delicious pie.

Hint: We recommend the use of Polaner's or other "all fruit" marmalade as opposed to the ones that have sugar added. If you prefer a sweeter taste use ordinary orange marmalade.

> 1 8-ounce package cream cheese
> 2 cups Cool Whip
> 2 large cans mandarin oranges
> 1 ready-to-use graham cracker pie crust (standard size)
> ¼ cup Polaner's orange marmalade

In a large mixing bowl combine the cream cheese and marmalade then blend well. Stir in the Cool Whip until well mixed. Cover the bottom of the pie crust with one layer of orange pieces, reserving another layer of the orange slices for later. Spoon in the cream cheese mixture over the top then add the remaining orange pieces to the top of the cream cheese. Allow the pie to chill in the refrigerator overnight. Serve cold.
Yield: 1 pie.

*FLORIDA-STYLE CRÊPES SUZETTE

If you don't have time to make crêpes, substitute purchased crêpes and serve with the Orange Topper. Or, you can make the crêpes up to 2 days ahead. Stack them with waxed paper between layers and refrigerate in an airtight container.

> 1 cup all-purpose flour
> ¾ cup skim milk
> ⅔ cup frozen Florida orange juice concentrate, thawed
> ½ cup refrigerated or frozen egg product, thawed
> 1 tablespoon cooking oil
> nonstick spray coating
> Orange Topper (*See* recipe, next page.)
> 2 tablespoons chopped toasted pecans

In a medium bowl combine flour, milk, thawed concentrate, egg product, and oil. Beat with a rotary beater until mixed. Spray an unheated 6" skillet with nonstick coating; heat over medium heat. Spoon 2 tablespoons batter into skillet; lift and tilt skillet to spread batter. Return to heat; brown on one side only. Invert over paper towels; remove crêpe. Repeat with remaining batter to make 16 crêpes, greasing skillet lightly as necessary to prevent sticking.

Fold each crêpe in half, browned side out. Fold in half again, forming a triangle. Place in a single layer on a baking sheet. Keep crêpes warm in a 300° oven while making Orange Topper. To serve, arrange 2 folded crêpes on each dessert plate. Spoon Orange Topper over crêpes. Sprinkle with nuts.
Makes 8 servings.

*ORANGE TOPPER

Try this sophisticated, no-fat sauce spooned over ladyfingers, angel food cake slices or cream puffs filled with frozen yogurt.

½ cup packed brown sugar
⅓ cup frozen Florida orange juice concentrate, thawed
2 tablespoons cornstarch
4 medium Florida oranges, peeled, sectioned, and seeded

In a medium saucepan stir together sugar, thawed concentrate, and cornstarch. Cook and stir until thickened and bubbly. Cook and stir 2 minutes more. Add orange sections.
Makes about 2 cups.

CITRUS DROP COOKIES

Each fall, this staple recipe was altered slightly in our family by adding 2 tablespoons of ground allspice to the dry ingredients. Growing up, it was a subtle hint that the season was about to change. A warm memory from childhood!

3½ cups all-purpose flour
2 teaspoons baking powder
1 teaspoon baking soda
¼ teaspoon salt
1 cup chopped dates, white raisins or nuts
¾ cup shortening
¼ cup butter
1½ cup brown sugar
2 eggs
¼ cup orange, lemon or lime juice
1 tablespoon grated corresponding peel
1 teaspoon vanilla
1 cup sour cream

Cream together the shortening, butter, and brown sugar and add the beaten eggs, juice, peel, vanilla and sour cream then blend the mixture well. Slowly mix in the flour, salt, baking powder and soda while constantly stirring. When well blended, add the nuts, dates or raisins. Spoon out the mixture in teaspoon size drops onto a large greased cookie sheet and bake at 350º until done (12–15 minutes).
Yield: 5 dozen cookies.

LEMON WEDGE COOKIES

Variety may be provided by adding 2 tablespoons of sesame, poppy seeds or coconut when beating in the vanilla, peel and juice. Continue as directed.

> 2 cups flour (all-purpose)
> ¼ teaspoon baking powder
> ¼ teaspoon salt
> 2 large lemons: 1 tablespoon grated lemon peel
> 2 tablespoons lemon juice
> ¾ cup butter or margarine (1½ sticks), softened
> ½ cup plus 2 tablespoons granulated sugar
> ½ cup confectioner's sugar
> ½ teaspoon vanilla extract

In a mixing bowl combine the flour, baking soda, and salt and mix well. In another bowl, beat the butter and sugars until creamy. Add to the butter mix the vanilla, peel and juice, then reduce the speed and beat in the flour mixture until thoroughly combined. Divide the dough in two equal parts. Roll in a log shape, wrap in waxed paper and refrigerate over night. If margarine is used, freeze dough overnight.) Cut first log into ¼-inch-thick slices. Place them 1½ inches apart on ungreased baking sheet. Sprinkle with granulated sugar and bake 12 minutes in preheated oven at 350°. Remove when the edges become lightly browned. Allow the cookies to set for 2 minutes before transferring to a wire rack for cooling. Repeat the procedure for the second log.
Yield: about 5 dozen cookies.

MARINATED ORANGES

The orange, one of Mother Nature's perfect fat-free desserts, is now available to us year-round. In the days when that was not true, our grandparents found a way to marinate them. Who are we to question their wisdom? Show respect for your elders and try them this way.

 4 oranges, sliced
 1 teaspoon orange blossom honey
 ½ cup water
 ¼ cup Grand Marnier
 ¼ teaspoon allspice, ground
 spearmint sprigs

Combine the honey, water and allspice in small saucepan and simmer, stirring constantly. Remove the pan from the heat when the liquid has been reduced and is syrupy. Place orange slices in a decorative jar or decanter with tight lid. Pour Grand Marnier over the slices, then pour syrup over all. Tighten the lid and roll gently to coat slices with mixture. Refrigerate for at least 2 hours before serving in goblets or over pound cake. Garnish with mint sprigs. **Yield: 6 servings.**

*FLORIDA AMBROSIA

Present this beautiful fruit mixture on airy meringue shells or angel-cake slices for a heavenly dessert after a heavy meal.

 ¼ cup sugar
 1 tablespoon cornstarch
 1 teaspoon finely shredded Florida orange peel
 1 cup Florida orange juice
 2 teaspoons lemon juice
 3 Florida oranges, peeled, sliced, and seeded
 2 Florida grapefruit, peeled, sectioned, and seeded
 1 cup halved seedless green and/or red grapes
 6 angel-cake wedges or meringue shells

In a small saucepan stir together sugar and cornstarch. Stir in orange peel and orange juice. Cook and stir over medium heat until thickened and bubbly. Cook and stir for 2 minutes more. Remove sauce from heat; stir in lemon juice. Cover; let cool.

Meanwhile, in a 1½-quart glass bowl combine oranges, grapefruit, and grapes. Pour orange sauce over all. Cover; chill up to 6 hours. To serve, spoon mixture over cake wedges or into meringue shells. **Makes 6 servings.**

*ORANGE PANCAKES WITH TROPICAL CITRUS SAUCE

Feature these fruity pancakes at a brunch accompanied with ham or Canadian-style bacon slices, assorted fresh fruit and frosty glasses of Florida orange juice.

¼ cup sugar
1 tablespoon cornstarch
1¼ cups Florida orange juice
2 teaspoons margarine or butter
1 8-ounce can pineapple tidbits (juice pack), drained
2¼ cups reduced-fat packaged biscuit mix
¾ cup skim milk
½ cup frozen Florida orange juice concentrate, thawed
2 beaten eggs or ½ cup refrigerated or frozen egg product, thawed
1 medium banana, sliced

For sauce, in a small saucepan combine sugar and cornstarch. Stir in orange juice. Cook and stir over medium heat until thickened and bubbly. Cook and stir 2 minutes more. Remove from heat. Stir in margarine and pineapple.

For pancakes, in a medium bowl stir together biscuit mix, milk, thawed concentrate, and eggs until combined. For each pancake, pour about 3 tablespoons batter onto a hot, lightly greased griddle or heavy skillet. Cook over medium heat about 2 minutes on each side or until golden (turn when pancakes have bubbly surfaces and edges are slightly dry). Keep hot while cooking remaining pancakes. Stir banana into sauce; serve warm sauce over pancakes.
Makes 6 servings (3 pancakes and about ⅓ cup sauce each).

CANDIED FRUIT

A great after-dinner treat to accompany a fruity liqueur.

   seedless red grapes
   seedless orange sections
   walnut halves
   strawberries
   2½ pounds sugar
   2 cups water

Spear alternate fruit types on bamboo skewers then place them on a
plate until all of the fruit has been utilized. Thoroughly mix the
sugar with the water in a small saucepan then on high heat bring the
liquid to a boil. Stir the mixture well then dip the fruit sticks into the
hot sugar mixture and place them in the refrigerator until the liquid
coating crystallizes. Serve these cold still on the skewer. Other fruits
such as pitted cherries, pears, peaches, plums, pineapples, figs, dates
and chestnuts can also be used.
Yield: 1 skewer per person.

NEW ENGLAND STYLE
ORANGE RHUBARB FRAPPÉ

Most people recognize rhubarb as a pie ingredient (its nickname is
pieplant). Its charming tartness, however, makes it perfect for all desserts.

   1 orange
   ¼ cup water
   1 pound fresh rhubarb
   ⅓ cup sugar
   ¼ cup soaked soft raisins

Wash the rhubarb thoroughly with cool water then trim off the
ends, and slice it into small pieces. Wash the orange then peel and
quarter it insuring that all of the seeds have been removed. Place the
rhubarb pieces into a food processor or blender and process. Once it
has been processed add the peeled orange pieces and process again.
Combine the blended mixture with the remaining ingredients in a
large saucepan, bring to a boil, then reduce to simmer for about 5
minutes. Allow the mixture to cool. Chill before serving.
Yield: 4 servings

CANDIED ORANGE RIND

Opposites attract! The tangy zesty taste of citrus rind with a coating of super-sweet crystallized sugar.

> 6 fresh oranges
> 1 cup water
> 4 cups sugar
> 2 cups water
> ½ cup sugar

Wash the oranges well under cool running water. Cut each orange into quarters lengthwise and remove the pulp with a spoon or by peeling. Place the peels in a pressure cooker with 1 cup of water and cook under pressure for 6 minutes. Cool the cooker instantly under cold running water to cease cooking then drain the orange peels. Remove the soft inner white membrane from the orange peels with a spoon, then slice the peels into ½ inch strips and return them to the pressure cooker. Add 4 cups of sugar and 2 cups of water to the cooker and mix well. Cook under pressure for 1 additional minute then allow the pressure inside the cooker to drop gradually of its own accord. Once pressure has dissipated drain the peels and dry them on a paper towel. Roll the peels in ½ cup of sugar and place them on a broiler rack. Place the rack in the oven at very low heat until the peels become crisp. Allow them to cool before serving.

*FLORIDA ORANGE DATE NUT BRAN MUFFINS

2 cups shredded bran cereal
¾ cup boiling water
¼ cup vegetable oil
¾ cup buttermilk
¼ cup Florida orange juice
2 tablespoons dark molasses
2 tablespoons honey
1 tablespoon grated orange zest
1 large egg (egg substitute optional)
¾ cup all-purpose flour
½ cup whole wheat flour
1½ teaspoons baking soda
½ teaspoon salt
1 cup chopped dates
¾ cup chopped walnuts

Heat oven to 400°. Grease one 12-cup muffin tin. In a large bowl, combine bran cereal, water and oil, stirring until bran softens. In a small bowl, whisk buttermilk, Florida orange juice, molasses, honey, orange zest, and egg until blended. In a small bowl, combine flours, baking soda and salt. Add buttermilk mixture to bran, stirring to combine. Add flour mixture, dates and walnuts to bran mixture, stirring just until flour is moistened. Spoon into muffin cups, and bake until top springs back when lightly pressed, about 18 minutes. Let cool in pan 5 minutes before removing to wire rack.
Makes 12 muffins.

*ORANGE-CARAMEL FLAN

1 tablespoon lemon juice
¼ cup water
3 cups granulated sugar, divided
1 pound cream cheese, softened
¾ teaspoon vanilla extract
4 tablespoons honey
8 eggs
1 quart Florida orange juice
fresh berries as needed
4 cups Florida orange sections
toasted sliced almonds, as needed

In a saucepan, combine the lemon juice, water and 2 cups of sugar, bring to a boil and simmer until the liquid becomes a very pale amber color. Remove the pan from the heat and distribute the caramel evenly among 12 7-ounce ramekins (2 tablespoons in each); allow to harden at room temperature.

To prepare the custard, cream the cheese, add the vanilla, honey and remaining sugar; blend. Add the eggs one at a time, blend and then incorporate the Florida orange juice slowly (to prevent lumps from forming). Distribute the custard equally among the 12 rame-kins (5 ounces of liquid in each). Place all into a bain marie(s) with ½" of hot water and bake at 325º for one hour and 10 minutes (until a knife inserted in the center of the custard comes out clean). Remove the ramekins from the oven and cool on a rack. When room temperature, place in refrigerator. Chill until firm.

To serve, run a knife along the inside edge of the ramekin, invert plate over the ramekin, invert both the plate and ramekin and remove the ramekin. Garnish each flan with fresh berries, toasted almonds and ⅓ cup of Florida orange sections.
Yield: 12 servings.

BEVERAGES

TANGY CITRUS ICE

Ice cold refreshment with plenty of vitamin C.

    2 cups crushed ice
    1 fresh orange, peeled and seeded
    1 fresh tangerine, peeled and seeded
    ½ fresh grapefruit, peeled and seeded
    1 tablespoon lime juice
    1 tablespoon of sugar (optional)

Place all of the ingredients into a blender and purée on high speed until the mixture is thick and icy.
Yield: 2 servings.

CITRUS BANANA SHAKE

A cold and delicious fresh citrus refresher with blended banana. For those avoiding sugar, honey can be used in place of refined sugar. For a fanciful presentation garnish the rim of the glass with a slice of lime and a slice of orange.

    ½ medium banana, peeled and cut into pieces
    ½ cup fresh orange juice
    1 tablespoon fresh lime juice
    ¼ cup plain yogurt
    1 teaspoon sugar

Blend the banana, orange juice, lime juice, yogurt, and sugar in a blender until the mixture becomes smooth. Pour into a chilled cocktail glass and serve immediately.
Yield: 1 serving.

NECTARINE-BASIL LEMONADE

Basil is perhaps best known as the key ingredient in pesto sauce, but its qualities are much more versatile. Its subtle lemon flavor mingles well with various fruits, and helps produce a lemonade that's out of this world.

> 3½ cups water
> 1 cup fresh lemon basil leaves (save additional for garnish)
> 2 nectarines
> ¾ cup sugar
> 1 cup fresh lemon juice

Wash the nectarines in cool water and remove the pits. Chop one of them coarsely reserving the other for slicing later. Place in a small saucepan 2 cups of water, 1 cup of basil, the chopped nectarine, and the sugar, then bring the mixture to a boil, stirring until the sugar is thoroughly dissolved. Allow the hot mixture to simmer for approximately 5 minutes. After the mixture has cooled pour it through a strainer into a serving pitcher. Slice the remaining nectarine into thin wedges and add it to the mixture along with the remaining 1½ cups of water and the cup of lemon juice. Stir the mixture well and pour it over ice into tall glasses. Garnish the tops with a few sprigs of basil. **Yield: Serves 4 to 6.**

SMOOTHIE MINTY LIMEADE

A treat for children of the south in times past becomes a pleasure enjoyed by us all in the present.

> ½ cup sugar
> 1 cup water
> 6 limes, squeezed
> 1 quart club soda
> crushed ice
> 8 sprigs spearmint

Reserve ¼ cup of sugar in a saucer. Dissolve ¼ cup sugar in water, club soda, and lime juice. Rub the rims of frosted glasses with a lime wedge. Swirl frosted glasses through the sugar in a saucer, until the rim is sugar coated. Pour limeade over crushed ice and garnish with spearmint sprigs. **Yield: 8 servings.**

SPICED WINE AU CANADA

Remember that boiling affects flavor of lemon juice. Heat gently! Makes a wonderful hot drink for the holidays.

> 1 quart water
> 3 cups sugar
> spice bag—12 cloves, 4 sticks cinnamon, 6 whole allspice,
>   and ½ teaspoon powdered ginger
> 2 tablespoons zest each, lemon and orange
> 2 cups orange juice
> 1 cup lemon juice
> 1 pint claret or light chianti

In a medium saucepan, combine together the water, sugar, citrus zests and spice bag, then bring to a boil, stirring until all sugar is dissolved (10 minutes). Remove from the heat and put aside for 1 hour. Remove the spice bag and discard. Add juices and wine and gently heat the mixture. Serve hot in mugs with optional cinnamon sticks. **Yield: 20 servings.**

PATRIOTIC LEMONADE

The children in the family named this because of its colors. Not a bad idea for a July 4th or Bastille Day celebration. From the mouth of babes.

Hint: Try freezing rind or herbs in ice cubes and use them in drinks compatible with herbs or citrus, such as this one.

> ¼ cup sugar
> 1 cup fresh lemon juice
> 1½ cups water
> 2½ pineapple juice
> 1½ cups plain seltzer
> ½ pineapple chunks
> ½ cup blueberries
> 1 cup strawberries, hulled and cut in half

Combine together the sugar, lemon juice and water in large pitcher then stir until the sugar is completely dissolved. Add in and mix well the pineapple juice, seltzer, pineapple and berries. Serve over ice. **Yield: 2 quarts.**

LEMON SHERRY SYLLABUB

*A cold creamy beverage that brings compliments every time it is served.
To prevent separation, serve immediately upon being chilled.*

½ cup sugar
2 teaspoons grated lemon peel
2 tablespoons lemon juice
½ cup Spanish sherry
1¼ cups whipping cream
Julienne lemon peel (garnish)
Lemon-peel twists (garnish)

Combine together in a mixing bowl the sherry, sugar, lemon peel
and lemon juice and let the mixture marinate in the refrigerator for
1 hour. Slowly add the cream to the mixture and whisk until soft
peeks begin to form. Spoon the mixture into decorative glasses and
garnish with julienne lemon peel and twists.
Yield: 6 servings.

OLD-FASHIONED LEMON-ORANGEADE

After all these years, still a favorite refreshment.

8 large lemons
2 cups sugar
1 orange
1 quart water

Pour 1 quart water into a large pitcher and add the sugar. Stir well
until thoroughly dissolved. Peel the lemon rinds in thin strips and
add them to the pitcher. Cover and refrigerate overnight. Squeeze
the lemons and strain the juice into the pitcher. Slice the orange into
thin slices, and remove the seeds. Add ½ orange halves to the pitcher
and refrigerate for 1 hour. Serve in frosted glasses over crushed ice.
Garnish by slipping an orange half over glass rim before serving.
Yield: 2½ pints.

LEMON SYRUP

Do not attempt to use a one-step method as boiling lemon juice will affect flavor. Syrup is strong so only 1 to 1½ tablespoons per glass will be needed. Any citrus of choice may be substituted—lemon is our pick.

 2 cups sugar
 2 tablespoons lemon rind, finely grated
 ½ cup water
 1½ cups fresh lemon juice

Make simple lemon/sugar syrup by simmering sugar, water and lemon zest until the sugar is thoroughly dissolved and the texture is slightly thickened. Remove from the heat and pour in the lemon juice slowly in a steady stream. Stir and pour into an airtight jar. Refrigerate until needed. Pour syrup over ice, fill glass with tap water, or seltzer for fizz, stir and enjoy fresh lemonade, tropical style.

HOT BRITISH WASSAIL

Equally inviting whether served from a crock pot during the holidays or from a thermos on a hunting or fishing trip.

 1 gallon apple cider
 1 cup dark-brown sugar
 1 pint cranberry juice cocktail
 1 6-ounce can frozen lemonade concentrate
 1 6-ounce can frozen orange-juice concentrate
 1 medium orange
 6 whole cloves
 1 tablespoon ground allspice
 1 teaspoon ground nutmeg
 3 cinnamon sticks

In a crock pot combine the cider, cranberry juice cocktail, brown sugar, undiluted lemonade and orange juice. Pierce the orange in 6 places and insert a clove in each cut, then add it to the blend, along with the nutmeg, allspice and cinnamon sticks. Cook on high heat for about 1 hour. Continue cooking on low heat for 3–4 hours. Serve hot. **Yield: 24 servings.**

TROPICAL MANGO COOLER

    2 cups cold water
    1 cup crushed ice
    1 cup mango (cut into 1-inch pieces)
    ¼ cup sugar
    1 tablespoon fresh lime juice

Combine all of the ingredients in a blender and blend on high speed until the mixture is smooth. Pour the blended mixture through a strainer into a serving pitcher. Allow the pitcher to chill in the refrigerator before serving.
Yield: Approximately 5 cups.

PINEAPPLE & BASIL COOLER

    2 cups cold water
    1 cup crushed ice
    2 cups fresh pineapple (cut into 1-inch pieces)
    ¼ cup sugar
    1 tablespoon fresh lime juice
    few basil leaves, chopped finely

Combine all of the ingredients into a blender and blend on high speed until the mixture is smooth. Pour the blended mixture through a strainer into a glass pitcher. Allow the pitcher to chill in the refrigerator before serving. If desired, garnish with a basil leaf.
Yield: Approximately 5 cups.

WATERMELON COOLER

    2 cups cold water
    1 cup crushed ice
    2 cups fresh watermelon (seeds removed and cut into
        1-inch pieces)
    ¼ cup sugar
    1 tablespoon fresh lime juice

Combine all of the ingredients into a blender and blend on high speed until the mixture is smooth. Pour the blended mixture through a strainer into a glass pitcher. Allow the pitcher to chill in the refrigerator before serving.
Yield: Approximately 5 cups.

MINT STRAWBERRY COOLER

2 cups cold water
1 cup crushed ice
2 cups fresh strawberries (sliced in half)
¼ cup sugar
1 tablespoon fresh lime juice
few mint leaves, chopped finely

Combine all of the ingredients into a blender and blend on high speed until the mixture is smooth. Pour the blended mixture through a strainer into a glass pitcher. Allow the pitcher to chill in the refrigerator before serving. If desired, garnish with a mint leaf.
Yield: Approximately 5 cups.

PAPAYA COOLER

2 cups cold water
1 cup crushed ice
2 cups fresh papaya (peeled and cut into 1-inch pieces)
¼ cup sugar
1 tablespoon fresh lime juice

Combine all of the ingredients into a blender and blend on high speed until the mixture is smooth. Pour the blended mixture through a strainer into a glass pitcher. Allow the pitcher to chill in the refrigerator before serving.
Yield: Approximately 5 cups.

RED GRAPE COOLER

2 cups cold water
1 cup crushed ice
2 cups fresh seedless grapes
¼ cup sugar
1 tablespoon fresh lime juice

Combine all of the ingredients into a blender and blend on high speed until the mixture is smooth. Pour the blended mixture through a strainer into a glass pitcher. Allow the pitcher to chill in the refrigerator before serving.
Yield: Approximately 5 cups.

MINT, BASIL & LIME COCKTAIL

In the mood for a tasty but different aperitif? This is it! Cool mint, sharp lime, and the unique flavor of basil gently mellowed with light rum.

2 fresh mint sprigs, chopped
2 fresh basil sprigs, chopped
1 tablespoon sugar
3 tablespoons fresh lime juice
1½ ounces light rum

Combine in a blender the mint, basil, sugar, and lime juice and blend on low until the sugar is thoroughly dissolved. Add the rum and blend just until thoroughly mixed. Pour the mixture over ice into a serving glass. If desired, pour a small amount of cold seltzer water on the top. If desired garnish with mint, lime and basil.
Yield: 1 serving.

BANANA-ORANGE SMOOTHIE

Made only with low-fat yogurt and naturally sweet fruit. All taste— no sugar.

1 8-ounce container low-fat cherry yogurt
1 large ripe banana, peeled and cut into pieces
1 orange, peeled, white pith and seeds removed, cut into
    segments
8 frozen dark cherries
6 frozen strawberries

Combine all of the ingredients together in a blender and blend on medium speed until the mixture is smooth. Pour the blended mixture into frosted glasses and serve immediately.
Yield: 2 servings.

JUDY'S FROZEN LIME MARGARITAS

When cousin Judy attends a family get-together, she spends the majority of her time in the kitchen with the blender. Her margaritas are the reason. Her secrets? Rim the glass with fresh lime instead of salt and don't waste cold beer.

> 6 ounces frozen limeade concentrate
> 1 beer, room temperature
> 6 ounces tequila
> enough crushed ice to ⅔ fill a blender pitcher
> 2 limes, cut into wedges

Pulse ingredients in blender to desired consistency. Rim glasses with lime wedge and toss into glass. Fill with margarita mixture.
Yield: 8 servings.

Judy's Martinis: Place vodka, dry vermouth, twists of lemon rind and glasses in freezer 30 minutes. For each martini, combine 1-ounce vodka and splash vermouth in container. Stir gently, DO NOT SHAKE. Rub chilled glass rim with twist of lemon rind, toss into glass and pour in martini.

HOMEMADE ORANGE CRUSH

If you enjoy the intense citrus flavor of orange crush soda, this is your drink.

> 1 cup orange sorbet
> 1 cold fresh orange, peeled and seeded
> 1 cup cold sparkling mineral water

Blend together well in a mixer the orange sorbet and the fresh orange. Once thoroughly mixed, slowly pour in the mineral water.
Yield: 1 serving

BLACKBERRY LEMONADE

Nothing is more representative of the country life than fresh homemade lemonade. The naturally sweet taste of the blackberries saturates this favorite with flavor.

> 6 fresh lemons
> 4 cups water
> 1 cup sugar
> ½ cup fresh or frozen blackberries

Use a lemon zester to remove about 1 tablespoon of zest from the lemons then squeeze enough juice from the lemons to produce 1 cup of juice. In a small saucepan boil 2 cups of water and add the sugar, stirring it until it is all dissolved. Add the tablespoon of zest to the boiling mixture then pour in the remaining 2 cups of water and allow the mixture to cool. Place the fresh or frozen blackberries into a blender and purée them. Add the lemonade and mix on low speed then pour the blackberry lemonade through a strainer into a pitcher. Place the pitcher in the refrigerator and allow to chill for several hours. Pour the lemonade over ice into tall glasses, and garnish if desired with fresh lemon slices.
Yield: 6 cups.

BLACKBERRY LIME MARGARITAS

Sweet mellow blackberries and the tartness of lime combine to take this long-time favorite into the hall-of-fame.

> 2 cups fresh or frozen blackberries
> 2 cups ice cubes
> ½ cup fresh lime juice
> ¾ cup white tequila
> ¼ cup sugar

Place the blackberries into a blender or food processor and purée, then force the mixture through a fine strainer, discarding the solid residue. Combine all of the above ingredients into a martini shaker and add ½ cup of the blackberry purée, then shake the mixture well. Pour the mixture through a strainer into margarita serving glasses.
Yield: 4 servings.

STRAWBERRY RHUBARB LEMONADE

Summertime refreshment that's hard to beat. The naturally sweet taste of fresh strawberries is perfect with the pungent taste of lemon.

    3½ cups water
    2 cups rhubarb, trimmed and cut into 1-inch pieces
    ¾ cup sugar
    2 3-inch strips of lemon zest
    ½ teaspoon vanilla
    2 cups sliced strawberries
    1 cup fresh lemon juice

Combine the rhubarb, sugar, 2 strips of lemon zest, and the vanilla in a medium saucepan and, while constantly stirring, bring the mixture to a boil. Mix until the sugar is thoroughly dissolved. Reduce the heat, cover, and allow the mixture to simmer on low heat for 8-10 minutes. Add 1 cup of the strawberries, stir and boil the mixture, covered, for 2 minutes. Let the mixture cool, then pour it through a strainer into a pitcher. Stir in the remaining 1 cup of strawberries and the lemon juice, then pour into serving glasses and garnish with additional lemon zest.
Yield: 6 servings.

PINEAPPLE LEMONADE

The naturally sweet taste of pineapple was custom-made for the tartness of lemon. Together they result in the world's most delicious lemonade.

    2 cups sugar
    2 cups unsweetened pineapple juice
    2 cups seltzer
    1 cup fresh lemon juice
    8 lemon slices
    8 mint sprigs

In a saucepan combine the sugar with 2 cups water and bring the mixture to a boil over moderately high heat while constantly stirring. Once the sugar is fully dissolved reduce the heat and simmer the syrup undisturbed, for 10 minutes. Allow the syrup to cool then stir in the pineapple juice, seltzer, and lemon juice. Pour the mixture into tall glasses filled with ice cubes and garnish the drinks with the lemon slices and the mint sprigs.
Yield: 8 drinks.

FRESH MINT & GINGER LEMONADE

This distinctive fat-free drink is a great change of pace from coffee or tea.

½ cup (packed) chopped fresh mint leaves
⅓ cup chopped fresh ginger
⅓ cup honey
2 cups boiling water
⅓ cup fresh lemon juice
1½ cups (about) cold water
ice cubes
fresh mint leaves
lemon slices

In a medium bowl combine together the mint, honey and ginger then add boiling water. Allow the mixture to steep for approximately 25 minutes then pour it through a strainer and into a pitcher. Add the lemon juice and enough cold water to make 4 cups. Cover the pitcher and allow to cool in the refrigerator before serving.
Yield: 4 servings.

SHERRY LEMONADE

Ice cold lemonade with the gentle smooth taste of sherry.

1½ ounces medium-dry sherry
3 tablespoons fresh lemon juice
2 tablespoons superfine granulated sugar, or to taste
½- to ⅓-cup chilled seltzer
1 lemon slice for garnish

Combine together in a tall glass the sherry, lemon juice, and sugar, then stir until the sugar is thoroughly dissolved. Fill glass with ice and add seltzer. Garnish the top with a lemon slice.
Yield: 1 serving.

FRESH GRAPEFRUIT & ORANGE PEKOE TEA

A great tasting alternative to simple ice tea for those hot humid days.

 1 cup brewed orange pekoe tea, cold
 1 cup fresh grapefruit pieces, seeds removed
 3 ice cubes

Mix together in a tall glass the tea and grapefruit pieces. Add the ice and serve.
Yield: 1 serving.

MELON, ORANGE CITRUS MIXER

Cold and refreshing, but not too sweet.

 1½ cups fresh watermelon chunks, seedless
 1 fresh orange, peeled and seeded
 ½ cup lime sorbet
 ¼ lemon, peeled with seeds removed

Place all of the ingredients into a blender and mix on high until well blended.
Yield: 2 servings.

TORTOLA FRUIT SALAD BLEND

A blend of fresh fruits and ice brings images of those lazy tropical days under a shade tree.

 ½ fresh lemon, peeled and seeded
 1 cup fresh or frozen strawberries
 ½ cup crushed ice
 1 navel orange, peeled and seeded
 ¼ fresh grapefruit, peeled and seeded

Blend all of the ingredients in a blender until thoroughly mixed.
Yield: 2 servings.

TROPICAL FOUR FRUITS WITH MAPLE SYRUP

The delicate combination of four different fruits give this special beverage its name. The taste can be varied by substituting honey for the maple syrup.

4 bananas, peeled, cut into pieces
2 cups chilled orange juice
½ fresh pineapple, peeled, cored, cut into chunks
1 cup cold water
2½ tablespoons pure maple syrup
2 tablespoons grenadine
6 fresh strawberries
1 tablespoon fresh lemon juice

Combine the bananas and ¼ cup of the orange juice in a blender and purée until the mixture is thoroughly blended. Pour the mixture into a pitcher. Purée the pineapple and ¼ cup of orange juice in a blender and add it to the pitcher. Add the water, syrup, grenadine, lemon juice and the remaining orange juice to the pitcher and stir well. Place in the refrigerator for a few hours before serving.
Yield: 6 servings.

INDEX